Help Your Children Cope with Your Divorce

Paula Hall

relate

Vermilion
LONDON

1 3 5 7 9 10 8 6 4 2

Published in 2007 by Vermilion, an imprint of Ebury Publishing

A Random House Group Company

The Random House Group Limited Reg. No. 954009

Addresses for companies within the Random House Group can be
found at: www.randomhouse.co.uk

A CIP catalogue record for this book is available
from the British Library

The Random House Group Limited makes every effort to ensure that
the papers used in our books are made from trees that have been legally
sourced from well-managed and credibly certified forests.
Our paper procurement policy can be found on
www.randomhouse.co.uk

Printed and bound in Great Britain by
Mackays of Chatham plc, Chatham, Kent

ISBN 9780091912833

Copies are available at special rates for bulk orders. Contact the sales
development team on 020 7840 8487 or visit
www.booksforpromotions.co.uk for more information.

To buy books by your favourite authors and register for offers, visit
www.rbooks.co.uk

With thanks to *Parenting Problems 2* for quotes on pages 64, 86 & 87.
All research cited throughout the book has been published by The Joseph
Rowntree Foundation.

Relate is here for people who want to make their family relationships better.

We help people make sense of what's happening in their relationships, decide what they want to do and make those changes.

In addition to our respected and popular range of books, we have many other ways to support people. Our counsellors are trained professionals, and you can have a local appointment with one face-to-face, on the phone or consult them online through our website. We also run relationship workshops.

We work with couples, families and individuals. Our work reaches across the whole of the UK, where we are the largest provider of relationship support and sex therapy.

Find more relationship advice and information about our services on our website at www.relate.org.uk or call us on 0845 4561310.

Paula Hall is an Accredited Sexual and Relationship Psychotherapist, experienced in working with couples, families, individuals and young people, and has been a Relate counsellor for over twelve years. She currently works for Relate as a young people's and family counsellor and also works in private practice. She provides regular professional comment on divorce, separation and young people's issues to the national press, women's magazines, teenage magazines, websites, national and local radio and television, and runs her own website: www.FamilyTherapyOnline.co.uk

Contents

Acknowledgements

My sincere thanks to all the people who have helped me write this book. I'd like to thank Damian McCann from Pink Therapy Services, Nigel Enser from Warwickshire CAMHS, Angela Holland from Parentline Plus, Suzie Hayman, author and broadcaster on stepfamily issues, Nicola Harwin from Women's Aid, and Anna Bloor from the UK College of Mediation. A special thank you to Gillian Bishop from Resolution, who gave so generously of her time for Chapters 6 and 11. Thanks also to Kate Maycock, Peter Bell and Nick Turner of Relate who painstakingly read the manuscript and gave me their wise feedback, and many thanks to all the young people's counsellors of Coventry Relate who helped compile the quotations.

Finally I'd like to thank my children, who have taught me more about helping children through divorce than anyone or anything else ever could.

Paula Hall

Introduction

During the twelve or more years that I've worked for Relate, I have seen countless people struggling to come to terms with the end of their relationship. And for those with children, that struggle has been both complex and heartbreaking.

Every parent wants to do the very best for their children, and most would go to hell and back before doing anything deliberately to upset them. But the reality is that an estimated 300,000 children are hurt each year by their parents' separation. For most couples, the decision to separate is an agonising one, which everyone in the family will have to live with for the rest of their lives.

Research tells us that children are distressed by their parents' separation, but for the vast majority, the pain is temporary. In fact, when interviewed four years later, most describe themselves as leading perfectly ordinary family lives. We also know that divorce and separation are not single, one-off events to 'get through'. They form part of a transitional process that may last many months, and it is how well you as parents handle your feelings during this time – particularly your anger – that will directly affect your children. Research has shown that the key factors influencing a child's ability to adjust are the quality of contact with *both* parents and the level of conflict between them.

This book has been written to provide the guidance, support and strength that you will need to carry your children through this turbulent period. Part I focuses on the decision to separate, and aims to help you manage your feelings during this very difficult time. It also talks about how your children may react once the news has been broken. Part II concentrates on the needs of your children, and offers some practical advice for establishing new family routines. Part III looks at your ongoing parenting relationship, with suggestions for second families and those whose circumstances are more complex. Finally, at the back of the book, there is a list of Resources to help you find additional support if needed.

Throughout this book the words 'divorce' and 'separation' are used interchangeably. It has been estimated that an equal number of co-habitees with children separate each year as married parents, and of course the impact is just the same on those children. Although I have used the terms 'mum' and 'dad' and 'he' and 'she' to make the book easier to read, it is not assumed that all parents are heterosexual, or that all parents will be birth parents.

The book does assume that both parents will be co-operative in putting their children's needs first, but unfortunately this is not always the case. No two families are the same and no two separations will be the same. Some of the advice in this book may not be relevant to your individual circumstances, or you may be in the position where your ex seems intent on making life difficult for you all. In spite of this, I hope that there will still be plenty of information that you can tailor to your needs.

As you work through the chapters, please remember that children do survive divorce. Like you, they may struggle and flounder at times, but, as a parent, you have the power to minimise the negative effects and help them look forward to a new, happier family life.

PART I

The Decision to Separate

This section looks at the decision to separate. It starts with a chapter on the importance of accepting the finality of the separation, not only for the sake of your children, but also to help you to move on. Chapter 2 is dedicated to your feelings about the separation and how you can manage them and get support for yourself. Chapter 3 gives specific advice and suggestions on how to break the news to children. The final chapter in this section provides a breakdown of age-specific reactions to separation, as well as some advice on how to help each age group.

CHAPTER 1

Facing the Finality of Separation

Separation is one of the most painful and distressing events that anyone will experience. Many of you will be caught up in a whirlwind of overwhelming emotions, struggling to take on board the full impact of what it means. In particular, what it means to your children.

If the decision to separate was made some time ago, or if you're the one that chose to end the relationship, then you may have already reached the point where you're ready to move on and get the wheels of divorce in motion. But if the decision has been very recent, or it was a decision that was forced on you, then it may be hard even to think about the future.

Whatever your circumstances, the next chapter is dedicated to helping you to manage your emotions and to find support over the coming weeks and months. Later on in the book we'll talk about how to tell your children, how they might react, and how both parents can build a future where, in spite of not being partners, they can still be a great mum or dad. But first you need to be clear in your own mind that the decision to separate is final.

The first step to helping your children cope is for you to accept that the relationship is over.

Occasionally couples do have second thoughts. The reality of the split may have left one or both of you wondering if you should give the relationship another chance. If this is the case, then under no circumstances discuss it with your children until you've both made a firm decision about the direction of your relationship. Splitting up once is bad enough; doing it twice, and making your children go through it twice, is unthinkable.

ACCEPTING IT IS OVER

The first essential step to helping your children cope with your separation is for you to accept that it's over and there is no going back. Experts say the ending of a relationship is similar to bereavement. At first you may feel shock – especially if it wasn't your decision to split up. During this shock phase you may feel numb and empty, unable really to think or feel anything. Once this initial shock has worn off, it's common to go through a period of what psychologists term 'denial'.

There are two different types of denial. One is 'simple' denial when someone denies the reality of a fact in the face of overwhelming evidence. The second is 'minimisation' when someone accepts the fact but denies the seriousness of it.

Denial is a defence mechanism. When a person is confronted with something extremely painful, they tend to reject and deny it rather than accepting it. After a loss of any kind, a period of denial is very common (and natural), as a person comes to terms with the reality of what has happened. In most instances this phase will pass and you'll move on to the next stage of grief, but sometimes people get stuck.

People struggling with simple denial may tell themselves that the relationship isn't really over. They may persuade themselves that their partner will get over it. They may tell themselves and others that their partner's decision is irrational, maybe as a result of stress, confusion, a midlife crisis or a passing infatuation. In this kind of denial, people often find themselves making huge allowances for a partner's behaviour, accepting affairs or their partner moving out of the family home. They rationalise their partner's behaviour by saying it is part of the decision-making process, rather than accepting it as evidence that the decision has already been made.

Even if you're the one that wanted to end the relationship, you may still be stuck in denial. You might be telling yourself that you're going through a phase, that this isn't real, just a bad dream, and that one day soon you'll wake up and realise you don't want your relationship to end. Again, in spite of the evidence of your own behaviour, you might continue to think that maybe you'll be able to sort things out.

From the casebook

Neil came to me for advice and therapy eighteen months after he left Steph. The relationship had ended because he was having an affair with a colleague at work. He said he'd never stopped loving Steph, though living with her was very difficult. In spite of an incredibly acrimonious financial dispute that was still ongoing, he wanted to explore the possibility of a future with her. It became quickly apparent that Steph had given no indication at all that she wanted to resume the relationship. In fact, when I met her at a later date, she described herself as exasperated by her ex-husband's indecision. Neil was stuck in denial. He didn't want to accept that he and his wife were now moving in different directions.

Denial is very confusing for children. Even if you haven't told them that you're splitting up, they will still be picking up unspoken signals, and if one of you is in denial, they'll be taking in very mixed messages. When you do break the news, they need to see that the way you're behaving matches what you're saying. If you and your partner are literally saying different things – i.e. one parent saying Mum and Dad are splitting up, and the other saying things are going to be fine – then a child will be left feeling very, very confused and anxious.

As painful as a separation may be for children, not knowing what's going on is even worse.

Chapter 2 deals with the different stages of emotions (including shock and denial) in more detail.

ACCEPTING THE PAIN

When a person becomes stuck in the phase of minimising denial, he or she may find it impossible to accept the significance and the pain of the decision to separate. You accept that the decision is final, but find yourself saying that the split doesn't matter, that you don't care, that you knew it would happen. Or that you'll be absolutely fine and, in fact, will be better off alone. Or maybe you're saying that you'll still be great friends, and will still be able to do most things as a family.

Although it's important to be optimistic and hopeful for children, minimising the impact of a separation can be detrimental to a child's capacity to accept what's happened. The message may also be contrary to their experiences of other families' separations and what they've seen in the media. Many children, especially older ones, know that separation is painful and difficult. Telling them it will be fine leaves them unable to share their doubts, fears and the many painful emotions that they're feeling. Of course, separation doesn't have to be devastating, but the reality is that lots of things will change. Maybe not immediately, but over the coming weeks and months, life is going to be different for everyone.

If you're still in the place where you're not sure if the relationship is really over, take some time to reflect on these questions:

1. Have either you or your partner begun a course of action that would indicate that the relationship is over? For example, has either of you moved out or started a relationship with someone else?

2. Have either you or your partner taken any course of action to demonstrate that you want to save the relationship? Such as spending more time together, working at overcoming a particular difference or committing to reparative counselling?

3. a) Do both you and your partner have a clear understanding of what needs to change in order for this relationship to work?

   And:

   b) Are both you and your partner willing to work together to make those changes happen?

   And:

   c) Do both you and your partner have the personal capacity and resources to make those changes happen?

THINGS WILL CHANGE

Firstly, there will be many practical changes. Your finances will be stretched between two households, which may mean making some difficult decisions about lifestyle choices. You might need to think about a change of career or altering your current working pattern. Depending on whether or not the children are going to live with you, you may have to make changes to your working hours or location. For one of you at least, the separation is likely to involve a change of home. And as possessions are split, both of you will need to adjust to changes in how your home looks and feels.

Your social life will also be impacted. Without a resident childminder (i.e. your partner) you may have to reconsider participating in recreational pursuits and how often you go out with friends. By contrast, you may find yourself entering a whole new social network as you have more child-free time when the children are with your partner. Special events will also be different from now on. Birthdays, Christmas, Diwali, and other festival days – events often associated with family time – may feel strange at first. Holidays will require more planning, and there will be times when you may feel at a loss and wonder what to do with your new-found independence.

But the biggest changes to contend with are the psychological ones. Many individuals and couples struggle for a long time before finally admitting to themselves and their partner that the relationship is at an end. Almost immediately that the words are out – no longer a threat or a desperate plea for help, but a reality – the dynamics between a couple change. Regardless of whether or not the decision was mutual, from now on you are no longer partners. You will continue to be parents, but apart from the responsibility of parenting, your futures are now heading in separate directions.

Your relationship with your children will change. Rather than being part of a unit, Mum and Dad, you'll become two separate units. Your children will have one relationship with Mum and another with Dad. As a parent, the decisions you make and the lifestyle you choose will be more independent than you're used to. There may still be some decisions you'll want to consult your ex about, but on most issues, the responsibility now lies solely with you.

Your identity will also be different in your community and within society. You will tick the 'separated' box and/or 'single' box on forms. If you're a woman, you may cease to be Mrs, and when you go out to see friends or to school events, you'll probably go alone. You may feel as though people talk to you differently now that your status has changed.

The shift from being part of a couple to being single is often much harder than people anticipate. People expect that they will be upset and angry at this time, and they know they have to deal with the practical aspects of a divorce, such as the dividing up of property, or a decline in living standards (if only temporary, especially for men), but people usually do not consider the huge psychological impact of becoming single again. For some, there is a loss of self-esteem as they struggle with feelings of rejection by a partner who had previously adored them.

> **Research shows that children cope best with divorce and separation when they're able to maintain a good relationship with both parents.**

Divorce and separation is a very public event. In a relatively short period of time, it will seem that everyone knows you've split up. Once a upon a time, very few people asked each other about their personal lives; now you may feel that you need to give an explanation for the change in your personal circumstances.

WHY HAS THIS HAPPENED?

Searching for meaning is a very natural part of relationship breakdown. When we understand why something has happened, we can then begin to work through our thoughts and feelings about it. We can figure out who's responsible for what, and choose whether or not to let go of feelings of hurt and anger and move on. This process can take a long, long time, but if you've at least started on this journey, you're more likely to be prepared for the many questions your children will ask over the coming weeks and months. But more importantly, you'll be better equipped emotionally in order to avoid getting caught in the blame game.

One of the most destructive things you can do to your children at this difficult time is to throw blame at your partner. Even if you have no intention of verbalising your feelings in front of your children, the inevitable resentments that build up when blame is in your heart will leak out.

As already mentioned, research shows that children cope best with divorce and separation when they're able to maintain a good relationship with *both* parents. If one partner

Understanding why your relationship has ended can help you avoid getting caught in the blame game.

is being held wholly responsible for the break-up and the children pick up on this, then it's very difficult for them to maintain a healthy relationship with that parent without feeling they're letting the other one down. If you're serious about helping your children thrive in spite of your relationship breakdown, then you must find a way to develop a genuine understanding of what's gone wrong and what part each of you played in that. There are, of course, some exceptions – for example, when it might have been unsafe to stay in the relationship. There's more on how to manage this type of situation in Chapter 11. But in the vast majority of cases, it is possible to reach a place of understanding where neither partner is blamed. This is not an easy thing to do, and what follows in the next few pages is not meant to be a quick-fix solution.

As well as reading this chapter, you may find it beneficial to talk through what has happened with a trusted friend. Someone you know who cares about you and your family, and will support you as well as challenge you if necessary. Some people find that talking to a counsellor can be really helpful, as they can offer an objective perspective. It really doesn't matter how you work through the process of what went wrong, just so long as you do. Otherwise, the questions will continue to go round and round in your head, and the anger, bitterness and low self-worth may continue to grow.

SEARCHING FOR UNDERSTANDING

As with many things in life, it's often easiest to make sense of something by starting at the beginning. Many couples find that most problems have been around for much, much longer than they think. You may find it useful to get a pen and paper, and write a list of all the things that attracted you to your partner. See if you can cast your mind back to the first few months of your relationship. What was it about your partner's personality or character that you liked? Do they still have those qualities now and do you still value them? Or would you say that they have changed? It's very common to discover that the qualities which first attracted you to someone have actually turned into things you dislike, and either cause or contribute to the breakdown of the relationship.

For example, Jenny told me that one of the things she most loved about Kevin, her partner of eight years, was that he was laidback and easy-going. He was always happy to go along with whatever plans she made, and would throw himself wholeheartedly into every activity she organised. As the years rolled on she became increasingly frustrated at his lack of direction in his career and at what she described as his inability to make decisions. She felt that rather than being a mother of their two children, she was actually a mother of three. Kevin hadn't changed since the day they'd got together but as life had changed, she had expected that he would, too. She said she'd felt like a single parent for so many years that the decision actually to become one had been fairly easy.

Sometimes people change a lot. It may be that your partner is not the same person that you fell in love with, and the things you loved about them don't exist any more, or have been drowned out by other qualities that you find less attractive. Perhaps you're the one that has changed. If you cast your mind back to the time when you first met, what were you like? How would you describe your personality? What were the most important things in your life then? What were your ambitions and your dreams? Have you changed in a way that your partner doesn't like, or in a way that means you no longer appreciate the same things about him or her?

AVOIDING BLAME

Everybody changes, and change isn't a bad thing. As we grow into maturity and experience different things in life, we change. For most people, change is inevitable and a good thing. It's part of our personal development and life journey. However, some couples find it difficult to adapt to change, or they feel that their process of change has meant they've grown apart. When this happens no one is to blame – but both are responsible for the consequences.

It's probably worth spending some time here looking at the difference between blame and responsibility. We sometimes use the words interchangeably, and though the differences in meaning are subtle, they are significant. *The Oxford English Dictionary* describes each word as follows:

blame • *verb* hold responsible and criticise for a fault or wrong.

• *noun* 1 responsibility for a fault or wrong. 2 criticism for a fault or wrong.

responsible • *adjective* 1 having an obligation to do something, or having control over or care for someone. 2 being the cause of something and so able to be blamed or credited for it. 3 morally accountable for one's behaviour. 4 capable of being trusted. 5 (of a job or position) involving important duties or decisions or control over others

The big difference is that 'blame' assumes fault and means that someone has done something wrong. If you think about the example of Jenny and Kevin, it wasn't Kevin's 'fault' that he was laidback and easy-going. And it wasn't Jenny's 'fault' that she needed something else when they had children. Both have to accept responsibility for their inability to adapt to and work through their differences, but neither has done anything 'wrong'.

> *One of the most destructive things you can do to your children is throw blame at your partner.*

At the end of the day, most of us accept that people and life change, and, as a result, relationships have to change as well. All relationships will hit rocky patches and difficulties, and many people will be tempted to think that the grass may be greener elsewhere. Each of us must accept responsibility for the choices we make when we or our partners change. Whether we choose to adapt to the changes, fight against them or ignore them is totally up to us. Either way, we must also accept responsibility for the *consequences* of the choices that we make.

However, there are some instances when we might feel that our partner, or perhaps ourselves, are very clearly 'to blame'. For instance, when there's been an affair or another major breach of trust. In these cases society supports us in saying that they have done something 'wrong', but often the event is not the reason for the breakdown. Affairs are nearly always a symptom of an unresolved problem that has been going on for some time. That may be a problem within the relationship or the individual. Often something has changed and the consequence is an affair or another damaging type of behaviour. And while the affair may be the final straw that ended the relationship, it's important for you to also understand what led up to it.

From the casebook

When Marion came to see me she was devastated. Peter had announced two weeks earlier that he had met someone else. After twenty-eight years of marriage and with three grown-up children, the husband that she had adored, and thought adored her, had left her. She had no idea what had gone wrong. Over the coming weeks we explored the history of the relationship, and she became increasingly aware that over the past few years things had begun to go downhill. In particular she remembered Peter getting increasingly frustrated with work and anxious about a number of minor health issues, and on reflection Marion decided she hadn't been very supportive. She began to suspect that the affair was Peter's way of recapturing his lost youth. She continued to be angry with him for not giving her or their marriage a chance, but she accepted responsibility for not taking him more seriously. She would never know if the story would have ended differently if she had, but she knew that his decision was final and the reasons their marriage had failed were more complicated than she'd originally thought.

The pain of separation often fogs our ability to see the whole of the situation. On the surface, the reasons for breakdown may be obvious. Fuelled by our own anguish, anger and disappointment, it's natural to settle for the easy explanation, the one that makes us feel better about ourselves and begins 'it's your fault because'. But the real reasons are nearly always much more complex.

Focusing on 'why has this happened to our relationship' rather than 'why has this happened to me' will help you to look more objectively and to see the bigger picture. The exercise that follows may help you to work through some of the history of your relationship, and begin to form a healthier and more productive understanding of what went wrong.

For the sake of your children, as well as your own emotional well-being, try to find a way of letting go of blame.

The following questions can help you to reflect on some of the changes that have taken place in your relationship and the choices that you made:

1. How have I changed since we first got together?

2. How has my partner changed since we first got together?

3. How has our lifestyle changed since we got together?

4. How have these changes affected our relationship?

5. Are there any ways I could have avoided or minimised the impact of some of these changes on our relationship?

6. What could I have done differently that might have helped us manage these changes?

7. If, in hindsight, the differences would always have been irreconcilable, is there anything I could have done differently that might have avoided the break-up, without damaging how I feel about myself.

There's no doubt that in a small percentage of relationship breakdowns, there really is nothing that one person could have done to prevent it. You may have given 100 per cent to your partner and to your relationship, and you might have been ready and willing to continue to give 100 per cent to save it. It takes two people to make a relationship work, and if your partner wasn't willing to do their bit, then your responsibility for the breakdown is minimal. If this describes your situation then you may be struggling particularly badly with hurt and anger, and you may be justified in blaming your partner. But for the sake of your children, as well as for your own emotional well-being, you still need to find a way of letting go of the blame. Doing this will take an enormous amount of grace on your part, but if you can forgive your ex for their weaknesses and failings, both you and your children stand a much better chance of being able to move on healthily and happily with the rest of your lives.

You and Your Feeling

I make no apologies for starting this chapter in almost exactly the same way as the last – separation is one of the most painful and distressing events that anyone will experience. Many people believe that the only thing more painful than divorce is bereavement, while others say separation is worse, because at least with a bereavement you know there is no turning back.

Either way it is undoubtedly an extremely stressful time, which challenges us in every way possible. Along with the loss of our partner, there is also loss of the dream that we will live happily ever after. You may also be losing your home, economic stability and regular contact with your children. By anybody's standards, that's a huge amount of loss. And while you're struggling with your own feelings, you also have to find the strength to deal with the loss your children will experience. This is why it's essential for you to do everything you can to look after yourself. The healthier you are physically, psychologically and emotionally, the easier it will be for you to help your children with their feelings. Later on in this chapter there's advice on coping during this difficult time, but first you need to understand yourself and what you're going through.

Psychologists say that the emotions we go through when a relationship dies are the same as those experienced when we lose someone through death. Many therapists use models of loss based on Kübler-Ross's grief cycle to help people understand the many emotions they're experiencing. We talked about this briefly in Chapter 1, but here we'll go into more depth.

THE FIVE PHASES OF RELATIONSHIP LOSS

In this model there are five emotional phases to work through. Although it is common to experience them in this order, the exact sequence and intensity will be different for everyone. The first phase is characterised by *shock and denial*. When the bombshell hits and the final decision to separate is made, the first thing you'll experience is shock. This is often experienced as a feeling of numbness and paralysis as the news sinks in. You may also feel disbelief or denial, when either the reality of the situation or the seriousness of the situation is denied. Once reality dawns, *anger* strikes. Anger at your partner, yourself and the world. The next phase is known as *minimising the pain,* when we try to work out how to avoid the inevitable pain of what has happened. As time passes, the full impact of the pain is felt and we enter a period of *sadness and emptiness* before we go into the *moving forward* phase, in which we start seeking realistic solutions and accept a new way of life.

How you react and cope during these phases will depend very much on your character and personality and also on your individual circumstances. No two people are the same and no two divorces are the same, and therefore there is no right or wrong way for you to manage the rollercoaster of emotions. How long it takes to work through the phases will also depend on the degree of loss you're experiencing. If it's been a long relationship, and for you a happy one, then it may take a few years. If it was a shorter relationship, or one where you'd been unhappy for a long time, it may be a matter of months.

It's important to know that this isn't a purely linear process. Unfortunately you won't go through each step neatly, finishing one phase then going into the next without a backward glance. The heart and mind are much more complex, and you may find yourself slipping back to a previous stage for no apparent reason. It's common for this kind of regression to happen if new information comes to light, or you've reached a point of addressing a particular loss. For example, someone may be moving out of the sadness phase into the minimising phase and then hears that their ex has met someone new. This might result in going back through shock, denial and anger before getting back to where they were before. Perhaps you're putting the house on the market, and find yourself going back to the minimising phase as you try to avoid the pain of the loss. Slipping back is a normal blip in the process but it's nearly always temporary, and you're unlikely to go back to a stage with the same degree of severity. If you can, just be aware of what's happening and continue to seek the support of friends and others around you, until you get back to where you were.

For many people, simply having a name for what they're feeling, and knowing that it is a normal and common response, is a comfort. It can also be helpful to know what's coming next. Identifying where you are in the phases of loss can also help you with your children. If you know that you're in the anger phase then you will have to work harder at containing negative feelings about your partner. If you're in the sadness phase then you may have to force yourself to be constructive in response to your children's questions about the future.

What follows is a deeper exploration of what you may be experiencing if you were the one who ended the relationship, if your partner ended it, or if the decision was, more or less, mutual. In some instances, a person may feel as if they were forced to end the relationship, even though they didn't really want to do so. (For example, if there was violence, a long-term addiction or another completely irresolvable difference.) In this case you're more likely to experience the grief cycle as if your partner was the one who left.

IF YOU ENDED THE RELATIONSHIP

If you're the one who chose to end the relationship then, like many, you may be surprised to discover that you're struggling with many difficult emotions. Society doesn't give much credence to how painful it is to come to the realisation that a relationship is not going to work, or how much courage it takes to make that final decision. Many people agonise for a long, long time before finally admitting to themselves and to their partner that it's over. Often the grief process will have begun before the decision to separate has been verbalised. You may have already experienced shock and denial that your relationship wasn't working, and anger at what may have felt like an inevitable and looming break-up. Others find they repeat the cycle once the news is broken.

SHOCK AND DENIAL

This phase is likely to be shorter if you're the one that initiated the separation, but it will still be there. You may find yourself saying that you can't believe you've finally done it, and you may feel temporarily immobilised as you wonder what to do next. This phase may also be tinged with feelings of relief. Relief that you've finally made a decision and no longer have to debate staying together or splitting up. A common way that the shock hits those who've chosen to leave is shock at a partner's reaction. In your mind, you may be sure that this is the right thing to do. You might be convinced that your partner has been aware of how bad things have been and how you've been struggling to make this decision. But many partners are not aware and react very badly to the news. Seeing your partner's reaction could well trigger powerful feelings of guilt. Even though you may continue to be confident that you're making the right decision, you still have to see and accept the pain that your decision is causing to the people around you. Guilt is a horrible emotion that's strongest in the early stages but in time it does decrease.

The denial phase is most likely to manifest itself as a denial of the pain and difficulties that your decision has caused. In order to avoid the pain of guilt, you might unconsciously try to tell yourself that splitting up is not going to be that bad. The reality is that it will be bad. But that doesn't mean that the alternatives wouldn't be worse. In order for you to be able to help your children through this difficult time, you need to accept the harsh reality of the situation that you have created and be ready to share in their pain as well as building a brighter, more positive future.

ANGER

As reality sinks in, you may find yourself feeling increasingly angry, either at yourself or your partner. You may blame yourself and be overly critical of your decision. You may start beating yourself up with regrets and if-onlys. Alternatively, your anger may be directed at your partner, blaming them for what has happened or feeling angry at them for not dealing better with the break-up. Remember that anger is a natural emotion and it's okay to have these feelings. But you need to check that you're not getting stuck in the anger phase as a defence mechanism. Ask yourself if you're feeling angry because you want to avoid taking responsibility for something, or because you'd prefer to feel anger than guilt. Or is your anger to do with protecting others from taking responsibility? Or, very commonly, is it a way of avoiding the sadness phase? While you're in this phase be sure that your anger is not destructive and making situations worse. This is a difficult time for everyone; being hurtful or resentful will not help.

MINIMISING THE PAIN

As you struggle with feelings of guilt and anger, you may find yourself trying desperately to think of ways that you can avoid the inevitable pain of separation. As the person responsible for initiating this course of action, you might also be trying to think of ways for those around you to avoid pain. Sometimes this can result in bad decisions, which may, in the short-term, seem to ease the situation, but will create extra problems in the long-term. There is no way you can circumvent these stages of grief for anyone, and all you can do is be as open and responsive as you can and be alongside others on the journey. If your mind is brimming with 'maybe I should' thoughts, talk them through with a trusted friend or therapist who will help you carry out a thorough reality check.

No matter how bad your partner may have been to you, they can still be a good parent.

SADNESS AND EMPTINESS

For the person who has decided to leave, this is often the loneliest phase. Others may assume that because you made the choice to go, then you won't be missing much. But of course this just isn't true. There will be many good things about your partner and your relationship that you'll miss, and if you're the one moving out, you'll also be losing your home and your children. Some people find they start doubting their decision during this phase. Remember that your feelings of loss are just as real and valid as your partner's. But the pain associated with that loss is not necessarily related in any way to the accuracy or rightness of your decision to end the relationship.

MOVING FORWARD

You will almost definitely reach this stage quite some time before your partner does. Your decision to separate may have come quite some time before you told your partner, so you may have worked through some of the loss phases before they even knew about it. This means that you're likely to get to the place where you're ready to sit down with your partner and rationally discuss the best ways forward for yourselves and your family, while they may still be struggling in denial, anger or sadness. Although it's frustrating when you're ready to be constructive, your partner is still in the midst of strong emotions and it is essential that you don't rail-road them into decisions that they might later regret. Where children are involved, it's particularly important that neither of you goes back on decisions that affect them, so don't make any until you're both ready. If you feel your partner is deliberately blocking you, then obviously that's a different matter, but before you tackle them, be sure that you're not being insensitive to their loss process.

IF YOUR PARTNER ENDED THE RELATIONSHIP

If your partner broke the news that they wanted to separate, you may have known that your relationship was struggling or you may have been totally unaware. Either way, one of the most powerful, over-riding emotions you'll be experiencing is powerlessness. This is not what you wanted. This life-changing decision has been forced upon you, and there is absolutely nothing you can do about it. Depending on the length of the relationship, the degree of awareness of relationship difficulties and the support network around you, you can expect to go through the full range of emotions associated with the phases of loss.

SHOCK AND DENIAL

When you first hear the news it can feel as though the bottom has just fallen out of your life. Like many, you may spend the next few days or weeks in a haze – unable to think or feel anything. The only words going round your head might be 'I can't believe it'. And in spite of the support of friends, you may temporarily find it impossible to think about any kind of future. This may be accompanied by two variations of denial: denial that this is happening; or denial of the pain it will cause. You may try to reassure yourself that your partner didn't mean what they said, or that they'll change their mind. You might console yourself with fantasies of them telling you it was all a big mistake and you'll be happier together than ever before. Or you might try to tell yourself that you're not surprised at all – in fact, you knew this was going to happen and you're glad it finally has. There may be some feelings of relief if a partner had been threatening separation for a long time, but that relief will be tainted by the enormous feelings of loss. There's no real way to speed yourself through this phase but the more you can be aware of your feelings and talk them through with friends or a counsellor, the easier it will be for you to reach a realistic, if reluctant, acceptance of what's going on.

ANGER

For the person who's been left, anger is a very understandable emotion. As you increase your acceptance of the situation, so your anger is likely to rise. Anger at your partner's decision, their reasons for the decision, and their unfairness in not giving the relationship another chance. You might also feel angry at yourself – that you didn't do something differently, or see the break-up coming. Some people are

You're responsible for making decisions in the best interests of your children, in spite of what you may be feeling emotionally.

shocked at the amount of rage they feel towards a partner, people who would normally describe themselves as calm and laidback. It's important to recognise that anger is a natural part of the loss process and something that is out of your control. However, you are in control of how you demonstrate that anger. Remember that your children still need a healthy relationship with you and your partner, and what you do now in anger could have a long-term impact on that relationship. It's important that you let out your angry thoughts and feelings, but, for the sake of your children, let them out with friends and relatives – not in front of them.

MINIMISING THE PAIN

As the anger begins to diminish, you may find yourself desperately trying to find ways of avoiding any more pain. You may hear yourself making pleas with your ex or trying to reason with them to try something new to resolve the relationship problems. You might also find yourself searching for ways to make the most of the situation or minimise the pain. Over the years I've had people explaining the perceived advantages of emigrating, getting pregnant, moving in with a virtual stranger or even joining a monastery as ways of minimising the pain. During this phase of the loss process, it's common for people to struggle with increasingly low self-esteem as they hear themselves saying they would do anything to get their relationship back.

SADNESS

For many, this phase is rock bottom. This is the lowest point when you may feel most despairing and hopeless. It's during this time that you particularly need the support and encouragement of friends. I know it's a cliché, but it is true:

you will get over this and you will be okay. Unfortunately, now, when you need to hear this most, is often also the time when you're least able to believe it. Typically women stay stuck in the sadness phase longer than men, and men are more likely to stay stuck in anger. This is in part a product of our emotional hormones but also due to the messages we pick up from society. Even in today's enlightened times, it's still more acceptable for women to cry and men to shout, but ideally, you need to feel free to let yourself do both.

MOVING FORWARD

Whether you're male or female, the tears will pass, and you'll be relieved to find yourself beginning to talk about how you'll cope and what you'll do in the future. Some people might reach this stage fairly quickly and worry that they're getting over it too fast. Either they begin to doubt their feelings for their ex, or they may feel their partner is getting off too lightly if they move on too quickly. Remember that this is about you and your children. We are all different and recover at varying speeds. If your head and heart are moving on, be grateful and let them.

IF THE DECISION WAS MORE OR LESS MUTUAL

For some couples the decision to separate is reached together. It may be that one person chose to finally voice it, but both knew it was coming and understood why. You may have taken a long time to make this decision so could have experienced some of the grief cycle already. Indeed, you may have shared some of the process with each other, talking about why it's not working and sharing the pain of the decision. One of the hardest things for people in this situation to come to terms with is that you have to continue the rest of the grief cycle alone.

SHOCK AND DENIAL

You may feel as though you shouldn't be shocked – after all, you both knew this was going to happen. But once the decision is final, it will still take time for the news to sink in. The denial you're likely to experience is that separating won't hurt too much and you'll still be able to be good friends. Unfortunately the fantasy of preserving a sincere friendship is usually a way of maintaining dependence and avoiding the pain of loss. Sooner or later, one or both of you will begin to create the necessary distance for you to rebuild independent lives, and then the full weight of your loss will hit you.

ANGER

You will probably experience less anger as long as you both behave as expected during the break-up. Unfortunately many 'amicable' break-ups become less so once the practicalities are being worked out. Arguments about the children or money or the introduction of a new partner can trigger the inevitable anger of the grief cycle. Try to remember that you may be over-reacting to things at the moment because you're still grieving.

MINIMISING THE PAIN

Because things are basically okay between the two of you, it's easy to get stuck in the minimising phase. Rather than accepting the pain of loss and the reality of being alone, you may both find yourselves getting locked into conversations about last-ditch attempts to resolve your differences. Make sure you both have separate friends you can talk to who won't be afraid to challenge you and bring you back down to earth if and when necessary.

SADNESS

The loneliness and emptiness of this phase can come as quite a shock. You may find yourself wondering why you're feeling like this when you both agreed it was the right thing to do. Be kind to yourself. Remember that you're losing a dream as well as someone you once loved very much.

MOVING FORWARD

You may find yourself feeling resentful if your partner gets to this stage before you, or guilty if you get there before them. Depending on your previous experiences of loss, your support network and your circumstances, you and your ex will go through the loss phases at different speeds. It's important that you accept that you are two different individuals and are now on different paths.

OTHER COMMON EMOTIONS

As well as the common emotions experienced at the time of separation, there are others specific to the break-up of a family. When you have children, there is an additional layer of responsibility. And with that responsibility comes anxiety about your children and how they'll manage both practically and emotionally. Consequently, many parents will also experience, to a lesser or greater degree, feelings of guilt and fear.

GUILT

Both those who leave and those who are left are likely to experience guilt. If you chose to end the relationship, then you may feel overwhelmed with guilt about how the children will cope. If you're also the one who continues to live with the children, then you're likely to be the one who sees their pain and suffering. Hugging your children as they cry themselves to sleep because they miss their mum or dad is heart-wrenching – particularly if you hold yourself responsible for the other parent's absence. And if it was your partner's decision to leave, then you may beat yourself up for not having done something to make them stay. As with all emotions, the pain of guilt will fade. In the meantime, get the support of friends and family, and remember that your children will get through this. Staying with your ex would not have guaranteed that they'd be any happier – especially in the long run. Unfortunately, guilt can easily turn to anger. If this happens, remember not to blame your partner in front of your children. They need to know that it's okay to love you both equally.

FEAR

Fear is one of nature's primary emotions and one of the hardest to rationalise. As well as feeling fear about your own future, you may feel intense fear about your children. You may be terrified of hurting them emotionally, losing contact with them or damaging your relationship with them. Like most parents, you'll probably see your children as the most precious things in your life, so the fear of losing them in any sense can be profound. It is a natural emotion, but remember that you do have the power and the resources to ensure that your relationship with your children survives. As the coming weeks and months pass, and you see your children coping and your relationship with them continuing, your confidence will return. However, if your fear is specifically associated with your ex's behaviour or threats, then see Chapter 11.

As I've already said, we are all unique individuals. You may experience the phases and emotions described above in a completely different order, or you may not feel any of them at all. Some days you may feel as if you're suffering from all of the emotions at once. Humans are complex, and what's most important is that you allow yourself to be you. You'll find more on your feelings in Chapters 7 and 8.

SEPARATING PERSONAL EMOTIONS FROM PARENTAL RESPONSIBILITIES

If you've ever experienced a close bereavement you'll know that a common and wise bit of advice is not to make any changes or major decisions for at least twelve months. The reason for this is that at times of high emotion, we're least able to access the rational, thinking part of our brain and are therefore more likely to do things that we'll later regret. Unfortunately, this isn't possible after a divorce or separation. There will be significant and serious decisions that you have to make. Decisions that will affect not only you, but also your children. You are responsible, as a parent, to ensure that those decisions are made in the best interests of your children, in spite of what you may be feeling emotionally. When we feel let down, mistreated, rejected or humiliated, it's hard not to let those feelings cloud our judgement. Similarly, if you're struggling with guilt or low self-esteem, your judgement will also be seriously impaired.

The bottom line is that unless your children have been abused, they need to maintain a healthy relationship with both you and your ex. And you have the power to make that relationship easy, difficult or downright impossible. If your children are also feeling angry and hurt, they might be saying they don't want a relationship with you or your ex, but still it's within your control to create an environment where they can change their mind, or you can increase the risk that they'll lose a parent for ever.

For your children's sake, make the time to cry and shout and share your feelings, but separate it from the time when you have to make decisions that affect your children's future. Take advice from family and friends – ask them to make sure you're doing what's best for your kids. I know it's really, really difficult to separate emotions from responsibilities – but not doing so has long, far-reaching implications for your children.

HOW TO COPE

Below is some advice that can help you through this difficult time. Remember that everyone is different, so you need to find the ways that work for you. Use all the resources that you can and remember that however painful this may feel now, it *will* get better and you *will* move on.

1. Talk
A problem shared really is a problem halved. It doesn't matter who you talk to – a trusted friend, family member or neighbour. Talking prevents isolation and puts us in touch with the many other people who've been in the same situation.

2. Get help
If each day seems to be getting harder rather than better, then you may find it helpful to make an appointment to see a Relate counsellor. Remember, many, many people need some extra help at this crucial stage in their life. You are not alone.

3. Let yourself cry

There will be some days when you just want to give up and cry. And that's okay. You need to be real about how you feel and give yourself permission to express those emotions. And when you're angry, let out those feelings, too. Keeping powerful feelings bottled up tends to make things much worse and can stop you from moving forward.

4. Look after your health

It can be tempting to indulge in comfort food and slump on the sofa all day, but this will just add to negative feelings. Taking regular exercise and maintaining a healthy diet can help your body and mind to feel better.

5. Set small goals

When times are tough you may feel as if you're getting nowhere. Setting yourself small, achievable goals not only boosts feel-good chemicals (endorphins), but self-confidence, too. Whether it's getting a chore out of the way, going out for the evening or starting a new work project, it will help you to see and know that you're moving on.

6. Plan ahead

Sometimes it may feel as if you'll never get over this break-up, so it can be really helpful to plan ahead to the day when you *are* over it. Let your imagination run riot and plan all the things you're going to do.

7. Relax

Try to take time to relax. Relaxation will help your body to de-stress. You could read a book, watch a DVD, go for a walk, or have a soak in the bath. If you're an active person, go for a run, work out in the gym, kick a ball around or do some gardening.

8. Laugh

Laughter really is a great tonic. It may be difficult to find things to laugh about right now but keep watching comedies and getting your friends to tell you their latest corny joke. When you laugh your body releases its feel-good chemicals.

9. Treat yourself

Take any opportunity you can to give yourself a treat. That might be something as simple as a cup of tea, a foot soak or listening to a new CD. You could really push the boat out and have a professional massage, or organise a weekend away.

10. Get out

Rebuilding a social circle is difficult for anyone after a break-up, but with more and more people separating, it's getting easier. Join a yoga class, darts club, gym or local Sunday football team. Take up squash or golf, or bingo, or learn a new skill like pottery or plumbing or Portuguese. Anything that will get you out and meeting new people.

11. Start a diary

Many people find it really helpful to write down their thoughts and feelings regularly. It's also great to be able to look back over the weeks and see how much you have moved forward.

12. Be more careful

Apparently people are more likely to have accidents when they're stressed or preoccupied – so take extra care when you're out and about, or pottering around the home.

CHAPTER 3

Breaking the News

Breaking the news to your children that Mummy and Daddy are no longer going to be together is probably one of the hardest things you will ever do in your life. Even if you're both 100 per cent agreed that separation is the right thing to do, telling the kids can be heart-breaking.

Your children may already have some awareness that there are problems between the two of you. They might even have suspected that separation was on the horizon. But finding out that their suspicions are a reality can still come as a shock.

How you and your partner break the news is critical to how your children will cope in the coming days. It's essential that you take the time you need to think through what you're going to say and when you're going to say it. You'll also find it helpful to anticipate some of the questions you might be asked and how you will respond.

If your situation is complicated by an unco-operative ex-partner then some of the following advice may be impossible for you to do – however much you may want to. However, hopefully some of it can still be helpful. You'll find further advice in Chapter 9.

WHEN TO TELL THEM

The best time to tell the children is when you've both had a chance to think about what you're going to do. Your children will feel more secure if they know that you've thought through what's going to happen in the future. Working through the checklist in Chapter 6 (page 93) will remind you of the things you need to consider.

Many couples want to separate as soon as they can. If you've been arguing for months, or have found out that there is a third person involved, you may be tempted to separate at the earliest possible convenience. But please remember, this is a major, major life event for your children, and waiting extra weeks, or even months, can make an enormous difference to how they cope.

There is never an ideal time to tell your children, but there are ways of making sure the timing is as good as it can get. You need to plan it at a time when your children don't have too many other worries to cope with. This means avoiding times such as exams, changing school or a bereavement (including a family pet). It's also best to choose a time when life's everyday routines are as normal as possible. Therefore, avoid telling your children when you're decorating or having other changes around the home, or when people are visiting or planning to visit. And, if possible, avoid the long summer holidays and Christmas time when routines are often disrupted.

> 'Mum went at a really bad time for all of us – like in the middle of my GCSEs! She said she couldn't stand it any more. I know she's happier now, which is good, but I'm still angry about how she went.'
> Jan, aged sixteen

WHEN CHANGES ARE ABOUT TO HAPPEN

You should tell your children before any major changes in their living arrangements have taken place and as soon as it's obvious that your relationship is over and you and your partner are making plans to separate.

It might be tempting to try to hide the problem until the very last minute, but most children are more sensitive than you think and may have been picking up signs for a while. Denying there is a problem can leave your child feeling confused and distrustful, and may ultimately cause more distress. Some parents begin to make changes and pretend things are happening for another reason. For example, 'Daddy's moving into the spare room because he's got a bad back and needs a firmer mattress' or 'Mummy's staying away at weekends because of her work.' This is more likely to add to a child's feelings of anxiety, and when you do finally tell them what's going on, they may feel cheated and less likely to trust you in the future.

'Mum and Dad had been angry for weeks, and I'd heard them talk about splitting up. But every time I asked what was going on they said, "Nothing." When they finally told me they were splitting up I was angry that they had lied to me and had treated me like I was stupid.' Jonnie, aged twelve

If one of you will be leaving the family home, try to tell them a few weeks before it happens. This will allow them time to ask questions while both of you are still around, and to begin to come to terms with the reality of the break-up.

Conversely, you shouldn't tell them too far in advance. If you are going to be continuing to live together in exactly the same way for more than just a few weeks, then children can feel confused. Small children, particularly, may be lulled into a false sense of security and can then be very upset when things change. Older children may see the current circumstances as 'working' and challenge why you can't separate but keep things as they are.

WHEN YOU'RE READY TO GO PUBLIC

Don't tell the children until you are ready to go public with your news. Telling a child that you are separating but that they are not allowed to tell anyone will put them in a difficult and isolated position. Your child cannot be expected to keep something as big as this a secret. On the other hand, older children may be angry if they feel as if they were the last to know, so don't tell too many other people first.

Before you tell the children, think about whether there are any close friends or family members that they may want to speak to straight after you've told them. Let these people know either immediately before you break the news or immediately after. You should also make arrangements to let the school know as soon as possible so they can be ready for any changes in behaviour and are able to offer additional support. (There's some advice on how to tell others later in this chapter.)

WHEN YOU'VE TIME TO SUPPORT THEM

Once you've considered the broader details of when to break the news, it's time to think of the more immediate timing. You should pick a time when both of you will be available for providing comfort and answering questions. Make sure it's not too late in the day when children may be tired, and not when either they, or you, need to leave to go somewhere else, i.e. to school or work. The best time is probably early in the day at the weekend or a half-term holiday when they have time for the news to sink in before returning to school.

WHEN THE CHILDREN ARE TOGETHER

If you have more than one child, it's best to tell them when they are all together. That way they can each be confident that they've been given the same information and will find it easier to support each other over the coming weeks.

WHO SHOULD TELL THEM?

There is absolutely no doubt that the best people to break the news to your children are you and your partner together. This is a time when you need to set aside your arguments and disagreements and co-operate. The only exception to this would be if you knew it would be unsafe for you or your children to do so or if you know your partner will be deliberately destructive (see Chapter 11). There are several advantages to telling your children the news together. Firstly it lets them know that your decision is mutual, mature and rational. It also tells them that you have both considered the decision carefully and are committed to this course of action.

In addition, most experts agree that telling the children together sends a positive message about the future. It says:

➤ We both still love you.
➤ We are both still your parents.
➤ We are both involved in looking after you.
➤ We have both agreed to do this.
➤ We both care about how you feel about this.
➤ We both want to help you to come to terms with this.
➤ It's not your fault.

It's understandable that some couples find this very, very difficult. Especially if one of you wants the separation and the other one doesn't. But it's still essential that your children see that you are capable of holding it together and co-operating when it comes to looking after their needs.

If your partner has already left

If your partner has already left, you may not be in the position to tell the children together. If this has happened then you're also more likely to be feeling confused and *emotional yourself. However, for the sake of the children, you need to try to put your emotions to one side and do what's best for them. If possible, contact your partner and agree that you will meet up to discuss what to tell the kids and break the news together. If that's not possible, then unfortunately you have no choice but tell them alone. In order to help your children to cope with what has happened, you need to be as honest as possible about the situation and work hard at not letting your anger or sadness affect how they feel about your partner. Like you, they are likely to feel angry, abandoned and rejected. Your job as their parent is to give them reassurance and hope for the future, because you don't want them to hurt any more than they have to. If you haven't already done so, take some time now to look back at Chapter 2.*

HOW TO TELL THEM

This an emotional time for everyone involved, and it can be difficult to contain the many feelings you will be experiencing. But your children will find the news easier to accept if you are able to tell them in a calm and considered way. They need to know that this is a serious and very sad time for the family, but equally they need reassurance that everyone is going to cope. Getting the balance right is difficult. Completely hiding your emotions might leave children thinking you don't care or that it's not okay for them to show their feelings. But children can become very distressed by uncontrolled or strong displays of emotion. Seeing that even though you're upset you are still coping and hopeful for the future provides them with a positive model for them to follow.

> **'Daddy was really upset when they told us, but he handled it really well and I know it's going to be okay.'**
> **Samantha, aged nine**

Most couples find it helpful to rehearse what they are going to say. You might want to write it down so you can be sure you remember everything. Decide who will start the conversation, who will say what and who will answer any questions that they may ask. For example, John and Sheila, who had been to a Relate for Parents session, agreed that John would do most of the talking because he was going to be the one leaving the home and they thought it would be easier for the children to see it as a joint decision if he explained it. They decided that Sheila would answer any questions they asked because John was worried that he might get flustered and, because of her job, Sheila was more used to being put on the spot and might be able to handle it better.

> *It is absolutely essential that you do not blame or criticise each other in front of the children. They need to know that they can still enjoy a relationship with both of you, and that they do not have to take sides.*

Whichever way you plan to tell the children, you need to remain flexible. You can't be fully prepared for the questions they will ask or how they will react, but if you've got a basic plan it will help you both to stay calm and feel in control of the situation.

KEEP THE DOOR OPEN

It's important that your children don't see your talk as a one-off announcement. They may have many questions that they will want to ask straightaway, but they also need to know that they can bring up the subject whenever they want to. Make sure they know that they can speak to you both individually or on their own whenever they need to. Your children will appreciate it if you each take time on a regular basis over the coming days and weeks to check how they are feeling.

WHAT TO TELL THEM

Basically your children need to know two things: what is happening and why it is happening. The first of these questions is most straightforward, and the response should include the basic facts of the situation and a broad outline of the future. The second question is much harder to answer in a way that is relevant to your children.

WHAT IS HAPPENING?

'Mummy and Daddy have decided to live in separate houses.' This is the first message you need to get across. You may want to pre-empt it with 'things have been difficult for a while' or 'your mum and I have talked for a long time about this' or 'you've probably realised we keep arguing recently' – but you need to tell them you have decided to separate before they become too confused or their anxiety levels start rising.

It may be that one of you has decided the relationship is over, and the other one felt they had no choice. But whatever your emotions, your children will cope best if they know it's a joint decision. You may want to give them more detail later, but ultimately, whether it's a reluctant or a welcome decision, it is one that has been reached by the two of you.

Next you need to tell them exactly what is going to happen and explain the changes that will affect them. Will one of you sleep in another room? Is someone going to be leaving the home? If so, who? And when? Will they be staying in the home they live in now? If not, when and where will they move, and who will they live with? If you need to sell the home and therefore can't give specific timings and details, at least give some guidelines. For example, 'Daddy's going to move into Grandma's house in three weeks' time and we're going to sell our house so we can buy two new ones nearby. We don't know exactly when we'll move but it will probably be later this year after the summer holidays. You are both going to live with Mummy, close to your friends and school, and Daddy will buy a house near to ours so he can still spend lots of time with you.'

If you and your partner have been unable to resolve contact agreements, or if it would be unsafe for your children to have contact, then all you can do at this moment in time is reassure them that you're going to do what's best for them.

WHY IS IT HAPPENING?

All children, no matter how old they are, need some sort of explanation of why their parents can't live together. Simply saying 'because we don't love each other any more' is not enough, and could cause anxiety. After all, children might assume that if you stop loving each other for no reason, then maybe one day you'll also stop loving them. Another danger of not giving an explanation is that children may blame themselves.

From the casebook
Sean was fourteen when he came to me for counselling. He was in a lot of trouble at school, and was a very angry young man who proudly described himself as a 'born troublemaker'. Over the weeks it came out that he blamed himself for his parents' divorce when he was nine years old. He recalled how he used to get told off for being naughty and sent to his room. In his room he would listen to his parents arguing and shouting at each other downstairs. I challenged how he knew the arguments were about him. He said he didn't know, but had always assumed they must be. He plucked up the courage to talk to his mum about it.

Apparently she had no idea that he had thought it was his fault, and explained to him that they had always argued about money, since long before he was even born. Sean began to see himself in a new light. He decided perhaps he wasn't a troublemaker after all and no longer wanted to act like one.

Your children do not need to know exactly why your relationship has not worked out. Your golden rule should be to stick to the facts, and keep your individual opinions and feelings out of it. I cannot repeat enough how absolutely essential it is that you do not blame or criticise each other in front of the children. They need to know that they can still enjoy a relationship with both of you and that they do not have to take sides. Giving them too much information or blaming each other forces them to decide who they think was right or wrong. Children have an inbuilt need for fairness, and will try to rationalise things that may be beyond their understanding. So don't put them in the position where they have any choices to make.

Here are some good examples of explanations:

'Daddy doesn't love Mummy any more because we don't have much in common and don't do many things together. He has met someone else who he wants to be with and he is going to live with her in a new house.'

'Mummy and Daddy have different opinions on lots of things and this means that we argue a lot. We have tried to find ways to get on better but it hasn't worked, so we have agreed that we would both be happier if we didn't live together any more.'

'Mummy has changed a lot since we got married and now wants to do different things from the things that we used to do together. We still care about each other, but we don't share the same plans for the future any more, and we both agree that staying married will make us both unhappy.'

Under no circumstances should you say that you have reached this decision because it is best for all of you. Small children will be confused as to why it might be better for them to live with only one of you, and older children will know that it's just blatantly untrue. Most children want their parents to stay together, and unless there is violence or abuse, it is generally best for children to stay with both parents. You must accept responsibility for the fact that this decision is best for the adults. The knock-on effect might be that you're both happier and therefore become better parents, but you have no proof of that and, at this moment in time, it's likely to be of little comfort to your children.

It's often very difficult for parents to decide how much information is appropriate for their children. And, of course, it will vary on the age and maturity of each individual child. It can be particularly difficult where sexuality issues are involved. Many parents feel uncomfortable talking about sex with their children, and most would agree that talking about your own sexuality is especially difficult. If one of you is leaving a heterosexual relationship because you want to pursue a gay/lesbian lifestyle, then there's some specific advice at the end of this chapter.

MAKE IT AGE-APPROPRIATE

Your children need to hear the facts that are going to affect them in language that is appropriate for their age. If you have children with a big age gap then you will need either to say things twice, or in a way that they will all understand.

When Bob and Rita sat down to tell their fifteen-year-old son and five-year-old twin daughters, they decided that Bob would do most of the talking and Rita would act as interpreter for the little ones if there was anything she thought they wouldn't understand or if they looked confused. The conversation began like this:

Bob: *Your mum and I have decided to separate.*
Rita: *That means we're not going to be living together in the same house any more.*
Bob: *It's been a difficult decision.*
Rita: *We're both feeling very sad about it.*
Bob: *But we think we'll both be happier living apart. There've always been issues that we didn't see eye to eye on, and we don't seem to be able to resolve them.*
Rita: *We argue about lots of things, and we can't really be friends any more.*
Bob: *But even though we won't be together, we'll still be your mum and dad, and we will both always love you very, very much.*

GIVE BUCKET-LOADS OF REASSURANCE

Your children will require lots and lots and lots of reassurance. They need to know that you both still love them and will keep on loving them. And they also need to know that they will still see both of you on a regular basis. Small children particularly can worry that if one parent is leaving home, the other one might do the same. So they want extra reassurance that they will always be looked after and you are not going to leave them.

Even if they act as though they're okay with the whole situation, they have to hear you say that you both still love them, that they will still have a relationship with both of you and that the separation is not their fault in any way.

COMMON QUESTIONS CHILDREN ASK

The more prepared you are for your children's questions, the more in control of the situation you will feel. Some questions may be difficult to answer. Others may make you smile or even angry. Here are just a few questions that other parents have had to face:

➤ How often will I see Daddy?
➤ Who will come and watch my football tournament?
➤ Does that mean we can get a dog?
➤ When I stay at your house, Mum, will you let me stay up late like you do when Daddy's away?
➤ Will we still be able to afford for me to go on my school trip?
➤ Will we still go to Uncle Tim's for Christmas?
➤ Where will the cat live?
➤ What does Grandma think about this?
➤ Has one of you had an affair?
➤ Why are you leaving us, Daddy?
➤ If I promise to be really, really, really good for ever and ever, would you stay?
➤ What colour will my new bedroom be?
➤ Will this affect my pocket money?
➤ Why are you making us suffer for your stupid mistakes?
➤ Who will take us on holiday?
➤ How can you say you love us when you're breaking up our family?

➤ Do I get to choose who I live with?
➤ Who will help me do my maths homework?
➤ Will I get two holidays every year?
➤ Whose idea was this?
➤ Whose fault is it?
➤ Can I go now?

Remember, it's impossible to be fully prepared, and your children will understand if you have to say that you just don't know the answer to some questions, or don't have the words to explain. Just keep giving them reassurance and telling them that you will explain to them when you can. There is more advice in the next chapter on dealing with your children's immediate reactions.

TELLING OTHERS

You may be keen to get the news out to everyone you know as soon as possible. Or you could feel that you just want a few close friends and family to know, and you will slowly let others know when you're ready. But remember, the news of your separation will spread. Your children will probably tell their friends, who will probably tell their parents, who will probably tell other people.

Many couples have found it helpful to make a list of the people they need to tell and then decide who will tell them, and when. Some people may be offended if they find out through the grapevine, while others may need to know in order to avoid an awkward situation such as inviting you to the same party.

People that you certainly need to tell so that they can support your children during this time are childminders, the class teacher, form tutor or head of year. You might also want to add grandparents, godparents, aunts and uncles, and close family friends to the list. Once you have told these people, you may decide that there are additional personal friends that you want to inform and perhaps people at work.

How you break the news will vary, depending on who is closest to them and how much they already know about your situation. But remember, it is totally up to you how much you say, and if you don't want to go into personal details about the breakdown of your relationship, then that is your right. In fact, in order to protect your children and your future parenting relationship with your partner, you should limit that information to a trusted few.

Depending on the age of your children, it might also be good to ask them if there's anyone they want to know. If they spend a lot of time at a friend's house with their family, they may want them to know what's going on at home and prefer it if you tell them. There may also be leaders at regular activities, such as Brownies, karate or swimming, to whom they feel particularly close.

If you're leaving a heterosexual relationship to pursue a same-sex relationship

Undoubtedly this is one of the toughest dilemmas that couples can face. We live in a society where homophobia still exists, and many couples find it difficult to get the support they need from friends and family for fear of disapproval. You may still love each other very, very much but have reluctantly decided that because of your sexual differences, you can no longer continue to live as a couple. You will have the usual heartache and difficulties that any couple face when they split up, but on top of that is the difficulty of knowing what to say to your children.

Even if you're confident that your children, whatever their age, have an understanding of homosexuality, telling them that their mum or dad is gay may still be quite a different matter. Added to the usual feelings about parental separation, they may feel confused and angry at not being told before and worry about how their peers will react.

Damian McCann, of Pink Therapy Services, says: 'The central issue for helping children is the timing and pace, as well as being sensitive to what your child may understand and be able to take in. Sometimes one or other parent may feel tempted to force the pace, particularly when feelings are running high. It is important that parents separate their own needs from those of their children, and where there are disputes between parents, it is essential that they seek joint advice.'

This book does not have the space properly to explore the complex dilemmas of coming out to family, and there are many other resources that already do this very well. The key thing to remember is that, whatever the reason for separation, your children need to know you both still love them and will continue to love them, whatever the circumstances.

WHEN TELLING YOUR CHILDREN:

Do

➤ Be as honest and open as possible.
➤ Be calm and optimistic about the future.
➤ Say that you're upset/angry/anxious but don't get over-emotional.
➤ Reassure them that you both love them.
➤ Reassure them that they will still see both of you.
➤ Reassure them that it wasn't their fault.
➤ Be prepared with the details of what's going to happen.
➤ Be ready to answer any questions they have.
➤ Let them know they can talk to either of you about this at any time they want to.

➤ Make your talk age-appropriate.

Don't
➤ Blame or criticise each other.
➤ Make generalised promises that you can't keep, such as, 'You can see Daddy any time you want to.'
➤ Be surprised if they already suspected.
➤ Be surprised if they had not noticed you were having problems.
➤ Tell them to keep it a secret.
➤ Go into unnecessary details of your relationship.

CHAPTER 4

How Children React

Children's experience of divorce is completely different from that of their parents. Most parents will have at least an inkling that their relationship is in trouble, but research suggests that the majority of children have no idea at all. Some children may be aware that a marriage isn't happy, but they don't question that it will continue. Even where there has been significant, angry conflict, children are likely to look forward to the day when their parents amicably resolve their differences, rather than consider the possibility of divorce.

A secure family unit forms the foundation for a child's healthy psychological and emotional development. When that structure is removed, the impact can be devastating. As adults, we know that many of the changes associated with divorce will be temporary and a new structure can be put in place, but children, with their limited capacity to time-reference, will initially assume that the current feelings of destruction and devastation are permanent.

What follows is an exploration of the kinds of reactions you can expect, starting with the responses that are common to all children and then looking at those specific to your child's age. There's also some brief advice on how you can help, but we'll explore this in more depth in the following chapters. Of course, all children are different and no two children will react in the same way. This will be dependent largely on their age, but also on their awareness and their experience of family change. The quality of their relationship with parents and other significant people in their life will play a large role, too, as will their individual temperament.

REACTIONS COMMON TO ALL CHILDREN

For most children, the first reaction to their parents' break-up will be fear. Children of any age can feel profoundly vulnerable and alone. The family structure that they have depended on has collapsed, and their immediate response will be, either consciously or unconsciously, to worry about what this means for them. Children of all ages also worry about their parents. They will want to know that the parent who has left is safe and that the remaining parent is okay – especially if they're showing distress.

Many children feel a huge sense of rejection when parents separate. Even older children who can rationalise that 'Dad left Mum, not me' can struggle not to take at least some of the departure personally. This can lead to intense feelings of anger, often accompanied by righteous indignation. As I've already mentioned, children of all ages have a deeply rooted sense of justice and will scream, either overtly or inside, 'It's not fair!' They may reason, 'If you loved me enough, you would have stayed together.' Their sense of injustice is closely related to profound feelings of powerlessness. This decision has been forced upon them, and they can do absolutely nothing about it. Many children will act out this anger in a range of age-related ways, while others push down their anger for many years.

'I knew Mum wasn't happy – but aren't mums mean to put their children first? She shouldn't have left Dad till we'd left home.'
Sophie, aged fifteen

This strong sense of fairness also leaves many children struggling with divided loyalties. They still love both parents and want to be loved back. But if one is more obviously hurting than the other, or one is being openly blamed, then they can feel that they should take sides. But in doing so, they know that they will hurt the other parent and may risk losing their love.

Many children feel torn in two by their conflicting need to show their love and support for both parents equally.

Guilt is another reaction common to children of all ages. In a child's egocentric world, everything revolves around them. Not only will they ask themselves, 'What impact does all this have on me?' but also, 'What did I do or not do that made this happen?' Many children try to take responsibility. In part this also compensates for their feelings of powerlessness by letting them feel involved – though obviously not in a good way.

> 'If I love Mummy, Daddy will be unhappy because he wants me to love him most and he's on his own now.'
> Joseph, aged six

Finally, many children can feel intensely isolated by divorce. Even though 25 per cent of children are likely to see their parents divorce before they're sixteen, it's still an event that's rarely discussed in the classroom or in the playground. While parents are engrossed in their own individual and powerful emotions of loss and anger, children can feel that they are left to cope alone.

AGE-SPECIFIC REACTIONS

As you read the following, remember that children are different and your child may be more mature or younger than their years. Not all children will be going through the same things, and, if they have a good relationship with both you and your ex, and they have other people who can support them, the impact will be reduced. But the most significant thing you can do is to try everything in your power to get through this process with your partner with minimal conflict.

Another point to make is that there isn't a better or worse age for your children to be when you divorce. Some aspects of the event and the process are better at some ages, and some aspects will be worse. And perhaps it's just as well, as we rarely have a choice about what ages our children will be when our relationship ends.

UP TO THE AGE OF FOUR

Babies and small children are dependent on their parents for their total physical care. Therefore this age group can feel particularly vulnerable to change. A baby won't have the same understanding as a two-year-old, but will still pick up on the atmosphere and their parents' emotional state. It's common for babies to feel unsettled during this time and they may cry more, and be more clingy and irritable. There may also be changes in eating and sleeping patterns.

Older pre-schoolers, eighteen months onwards, will be more tuned in to mood, and might also pick up on particular words that have either been said directly to them or that they've overhead. However, because they're not old enough to understand the complexity of the situation, they tend to oversimplify and create their own conclusions. For example, for a three-year-old it is logical to conclude that if Daddy left, then Mummy can leave, too. And if Mummy stopped loving Daddy, maybe she'll stop loving him or her. Their tendency to apply simple cause and effect logic to situations can result in them blaming themselves for a break-up. Matt, aged four, spent weeks thinking that Daddy left because he knocked over his drink. On the evening that he was told about the separation, he had spilled his drink in the living room (where he wasn't meant to have it) and had been sternly told off. He thought that if he hadn't spilt his drink, the evening might have been different.

Because of the dependency of this age group, fear is the strongest emotion they're likely to feel but with limited words to express it, it may leak out in behaviour. It's common for children to regress to an earlier developmental stage – for example, bed-wetting, wanting a bottle, being scared of the dark. They may also be more clingy, not want to go to nursery, and take much longer to settle at night. They might become more aggressive, even violent towards siblings and friends. Because of their limited capacity to understand time and distance, they can get very distressed at the thought of Daddy moving out, or having to visit a new house. Reassurances that you'll see Daddy on Friday, or that Daddy's new house is only ten miles away can be meaningless.

One of the positives of this age group is that they haven't yet established a firm history of family life and consequently they are likely to adapt relatively quickly to changes in family routines. As time passes, they will quickly accept new arrangements as the norm, and may even forget how things used to be.

How to help:

➤ Keep routines consistent – bedtimes, mealtimes, visits, etc. – and, where possible, maintain consistency in both homes.

➤ Give extra cuddles and comfort, and treat regressive behaviours as casually as possible. Don't encourage it, but don't over-react, either. They'll catch up again when they're ready.

➤ Try to relax, and give lots of verbal reassurances that you and your ex both still love them, that you'll both still be there for them, and that none of this is their fault.

➤ Keep visits short and frequent to reduce time away from the familiarity of home and the primary carer.

AGES FIVE TO EIGHT

By the time children start school, they are much more articulate and are beginning to develop some understanding of the complexities of relationships. They may have friends at

'My dad left us because he couldn't find his slippers. Mummy hid them so he couldn't come in.'
Mandy, aged seven

school whose parents live in separate houses, and will almost certainly have come across different family groups on children's television. With a little more grip on reality, they are less likely to slip into fantasy than pre-schoolers in order to try to understand what's going on, but they still believe in fairy tales and, more than any other age group, may cling to the hope of Mummy and Daddy being reconciled one day.

This age group tends to struggle most with feelings of loss and fears of rejection. They will be particularly worried about losing the non-resident parent for ever, or being replaced by a new child in one of the families. They're also most likely to be tortured by split loyalties. In their still relatively simple world of right and wrong, and good and bad, they may try to take sides with each parent but feel desperately guilty when they do so. As with the earlier age group, their behaviour could regress for a while, and they may be irritable, tearful and difficult to console.

'I just want Mummy and Daddy to be friends.'
Jamie, aged six

The good thing about this age group is that they can begin to be involved in discussions about what's going on and can hold on to a sense of a future when things will be better.

How to help:
➤ Give lots of reassurance – verbal and physical.
➤ Explain things in simple language that they will understand.
➤ Don't blame your partner or be angry with them in your child's presence.
➤ Let them know that it's okay for them to love both parents.
➤ Keep routines as consistent as possible, including school.

AGES NINE TO TWELVE

Known as the 'tweenagers', this age group can find a divorce or separation particularly inconvenient and difficult to cope with. As they're launching themselves into their social circle and establishing their own identity, they can find the disintegration of the family structure particularly threatening to their fragile status quo. Consequently they are likely to feel intense anger, and this may be directed at one parent on whom they'll dump all the responsibility. This blame is fed by their tendency for black and white thinking, which means that this age group are most vulnerable to being used by warring parents as a weapon against the other.

> 'I pretend I'm happy so I don't make Mum cry. When I see Dad I pretend I'm sad so he thinks I miss him. I'm sort of happy and sad. Happy it's quiet at home and sad that Mum's sad. I try to cheer her up but it doesn't work. It's like I'm shrinking. They don't really see how I feel.'
> Lucy, aged eleven

They're also more likely to worry about the parent they perceive as struggling the most. As they begin to practise adult roles and want to be seen as being more grown up, they may want to take inappropriate responsibility for caring for this parent. Conversely, when they need to show that they're still a child, they may communicate their need for love and affection through somatic illnesses such as headaches and stomach aches. They may start engaging in more risk-taking behaviour, such as stealing or playing up at school, as a way of drawing attention to their needs for stability and control.

The good thing about this age group is that they're more aware of the financial and social implications of separation as well as having more experience of divorce in their social lives.

How to help:

➤ Maintain boundaries but continue to encourage them to become independent and create their own social network and support system.

➤ Give as much information as feels appropriate but don't blame your partner.

➤ Don't let your child become your confidante or take on inappropriate responsibility.

➤ Create an environment where they can talk when they need to.

AGES THIRTEEN AND OVER

If you've got children over thirteen then chances are you're already experiencing a range of new and challenging behaviours. One of the difficulties for parents of this age group is knowing when a behaviour is a result of the separation, and when it's 'what teenagers do'. In spite of teenagers' strong rebellious streak, they can still be very moralistic, and your teenager may not hold back in telling you precisely what they think.

> '*I just can't be bothered any more. It's their life. I don't care what they do as long as I can still see my mates.*'
> **Jake, aged thirteen**

They're also at the age where fitting in with their peer group is essential, so anything that might cause embarrassment, such as an indiscreet affair or a new relationship, can be felt acutely. Because teenagers are so much more aware of their own sexuality, they can find it particularly difficult to face the reality of a parent's sexuality. Knowing that parents have had marriage problems and are about to be single closes the generation gap, and can leave them feeling anxious about whether or not you're still in charge.

In terms of behaviour, teenagers are the ones who are most likely to want to escape the situation. That might mean becoming quiet and withdrawn, spending more time with friends, throwing themselves into school work, or experimenting with alcohol or drugs. Conversely, a few may become very clingy and try to replace the departing parent by taking on the role of the woman or man of the house.

Adolescents have more understanding than any other age group of how life works – or rather, how it doesn't work sometimes. They're most likely to be sympathetic to the situation and optimistic about the future, but since this is such a time of rapid change and growth for them, they can feel just as destabilised as the pre-schoolers.

> *'None of my friends' parents have split up. I hate having to explain why sometimes I can't see them cos I'm at my dad's. It's so embarrassing. Mostly I just lie so I don't have to answer questions.'*
> *Jayne, aged seventeen*

How to help:
➤ Remember that mood swings and erratic behaviour are usual for teenagers.
➤ Give them space to be alone if they want to.
➤ Be flexible about contact arrangements.
➤ Let them know that it's okay for them still to feel like a child, but also respect their right to be involved in decisions that will affect them.
➤ Create an environment where they can talk when they need to – but remember that they may prefer to talk to their friends.

DIVORCE IS FOR LIFE

Whatever age your children are now, you will still be divorced when they're older and, as they grow up, they will deal with their parents' separation in age-appropriate ways. That means that, as your child grows, they will ask more questions, and the way they react will be different from before. They will also begin to see things in a new light. An eight-year-old that takes the news in his stride may look back at the age of twelve and question what has happened, then begin to feel angry. Some people make the mistake of thinking that children 'get over' their parents' separation. They don't. They adjust, but that adjustment continues as they grow older and take on the information in different ways.

From the casebook

Sophie was nine when her mum told her she was leaving her dad. She left a few days later and lived with John. Sophie still saw her regularly and, a few months later, Mum and John bought a house together and Sophie and her younger sister moved in. Everything was fine for the next couple of years. But slowly, Sophie began to question what had happened. She learnt what an 'affair' was and asked her dad if that was what had happened. He confirmed that her mum had indeed had an affair. She grew increasingly angry towards her mum and ashamed about what she'd done, and couldn't bear to be in the same room as John, who had 'split up her family'. Through family counselling, Sophie was able to accept what had happened and move on to a better relationship with her mum and John.

'I have to say I didn't have feelings about the divorce then and I don't now... As far as I can see, the divorce hasn't been a big problem to me. Providing parents act properly, divorce shouldn't be a problem.'
Jake, aged fourteen

One of the great joys of children is that they're rarely boring! They can be wonderfully unpredictable, and just when you think you've settled into a routine, they'll have an emotional or intellectual growth spurt and start thinking and behaving differently. Children of divorce are no different. As a parent, your job is to stick with it and them. As their understanding changes, be ready to listen and talk to them all over again. To you it may feel like going over old ground, but to them it could be a whole new view. There's some advice on listening to your children in Chapter 5.

IT AIN'T ALL BAD

Undoubtedly some children have very few negative reactions to their parents' separation. For some it may have happened so long ago that they genuinely can't remember anything different. Contact arrangements may have been in place for so long that it just feels like normal family life. Indeed, it *is* normal family life.

Other children may have lived in such an unhappy household for so long that, while they still struggle a bit, those struggles are outweighed by the relief they feel at not having to live in a war zone. What's important for you as a parent is to be prepared for how they may react. No one knows your children as well as you do.

> 'The good thing about your parents splitting up is you get two houses, two holidays, two lots of presents and two lots of pocket money – oh, Mum and Dad don't know about the two lots of pocket money!'
> Jen, aged thirteen

PART II

Helping Children through Separation

This section of the book is all about how you, as parents, can minimise the impact of your divorce. The first chapter, Chapter 5, explores the most common feelings children express, and how you can manage these. Chapter 6 looks at a variety of new living arrangements and some of the pros and cons of each option for family members. Chapter 7 is dedicated to the emotions and practicalities of leaving day. In Chapter 8 you'll get advice on establishing and monitoring new routines during your first year.

Coping with the Fallout

So you've told them. It takes a huge amount of courage to tell your children that you're splitting up and, like many, you are no doubt struggling with some powerful and conflicting emotions. You may feel relief that you've told them, but also a huge amount of sadness. Telling the children somehow makes the separation real. It is a significant point in the process, a point at which it is much, much harder to turn back.

How your children reacted when you told them will depend very much on their age (see Chapter 4). It will also depend on how aware they were that the news was coming, and what else is going on in their life. Their response will also be influenced by how they've seen you respond to difficulties. Almost regardless of what age they are, they will have learnt something about managing emotions from both you and your partner. If you're a family that openly shows emotion then you're more likely to get an overt show of emotion from your kids. But if you tend to be quieter and more introspective, then your children are more likely to respond likewise. Either way, you need to remain aware of how your children are feeling and behaving, and be ready to give ongoing support and guidance.

The time after telling the children – building up to departure day – is probably the most painful period of the entire divorce process. Most parents struggle to find the emotional resources to keep themselves together, let alone muster the strength for their children's demands. But nonetheless, the coming days and weeks are a critical time for your children, and how you respond now will influence how they adjust to the break-up.

You need to do whatever you can to put the needs of your children first, and separate how you're feeling about your partner from what you need to do for your children's sake.

The first task is to maintain as much stability as you possibly can for your children. Firstly this means looking after yourself. It's difficult to be a source of strength for your kids if you feel as if your life is falling apart. Look back at Chapter 2 for more on this, and remember to get as much support as you possibly can from friends and family.

MAINTAINING STABILITY

Your child's life has just been turned upside-down, and it's tempting to think that routines just aren't important right now. On the contrary; routines are doubly important. That means going to bed on time, eating meals as you did before, sticking to household rules, and carrying on going to school or playgroup and out-of-school activities. Grandma should continue to visit on Thursdays and you'll still take them swimming on Fridays. And yes – they do still have to brush their teeth. What may change is that if you've done some of these things as a couple before, you will now do them separately. You're no longer going to be a family, but the home needs to continue running just as before. The reason for doing this is that it reinforces for children that life goes on. Outer structure can help to ease the inner turmoil, and what you're saying through your behaviour is: 'We're going to be okay.' That's not to say you're going to minimise the emotions they're experiencing, or that you won't have to make some allowances for bad or erratic behaviour, but you can still keep the basic foundations of daily life in place.

In this very early stage your children will need to have some kind of understanding of what's happening next. If you haven't already done so, then look back at Chapter 3, and also take a look at Chapter 7. Until children know what's going on, they may be anxious and ask a lot of questions. They may also become hyper-vigilant. Most children are shocked by the news that their parents are separating and, in order to minimise any further shocks, may make either a conscious or an unconscious effort to ensure they're kept in the picture. Some children will go so far as to spy on parents, hiding behind doors to listen to conversations, or even rifling through paperwork for information. The more facts you're able to give them, the quicker this behaviour will stop and the easier it will be for them to trust that nothing is being kept from them.

MANAGING THE WHYS

Over and over again you'll be faced with the question why. Why me? Why our family? Why now? Why don't you love each other? Why can't you work it out? Why don't you love me enough to work it out? Why did you marry in the first place? Why didn't you divorce before I was born? Why did you meet someone else? Why are you being so selfish? The list is endless. Depending on the age and maturity of the child, you may be able to answer some of these questions, but there are many that are either inappropriate or just unanswerable. As adults we know that life is tough, relationships are complicated

> *You need to do whatever you can to put the needs of your children first, and separate how you're feeling about your partner from what you need to do for your children.*

and humans changeable. As a consequence, many relationships break down and, to a lesser or greater degree, you're probably able to rationalise what's going on. But for a child, it's likely to be too difficult to understand. Often underneath the why is a deeper need – for reassurance rather than information.

Why questions often hide deeper questions such as: Will you both always love me? Was it my fault? How much do you care? You may think that you've already answered these questions a thousand times, but if the questions are still coming, in spite of your best efforts to explain, then you may need to answer some questions that *aren't* being asked.

The bottom line is that children need to be constantly reassured that:

IT'S NOT THEIR FAULT

The separation has happened for reasons that were completely out of their control and there was absolutely nothing they could have done to prevent it.

YOU'RE SORRY THIS IS HAPPENING

That's not the same as saying you wish it wasn't happening (though you might), or that it's a mistake, or that you want to change your mind. It's simply saying that you're sorry that this is happening to your family and that it's such a difficult time.

YOU KNOW HOW PAINFUL THIS IS FOR THEM

They need acknowledgement for their feelings and to hear that you really are aware of how tough this is. Again, that doesn't mean that you can or would change anything, but you can still let them know you empathise.

YOU LOVE THEM

It may be obvious to you, but it may not be obvious to them, especially now. You can never tell your children enough that you love them. Keep telling them that, in spite of the pain that's being caused by this break-up, you still love them and you have never stopped loving them.

YOU WILL ALWAYS LOVE THEM

Again, this may be obvious to you, but younger children in particular can worry about being replaced or forgotten, especially by the parent who's leaving the home. Children need constant reassurance that though a parent may no longer be physically available 24/7 – they will still always love them and always be there for them.

> *'Why did they bother having kids if they weren't going to stay together?'*
> *Alex, aged seventeen*

DIFFERENT REACTIONS

Not all children will inundate you with questions. But even if they say very little, the questions may still be going round and round in their head. However they respond, make sure you're getting across these very important messages.

What follows are examples of some of the most common behavioural responses from children and also some ideas for how to manage each behaviour type from Nigel Enser, a child primary mental health practitioner, who says: 'Have a look at each possible situation, as the ideas suggested may be helpful in several of the situations. Think about what might be useful for you and your child. Try to see things from their point of view; it can help to understand their behaviour. Consider their age, and remember that as children grow up they will often look again at what happened and try to understand it based on their level of development. This means you may need to revisit issues with them as time goes by.'

THE SILENT CHILD

On hearing that their parents are splitting up, some children will withdraw into silence. Teenage children are especially likely to do this, as are those who tend to be quiet by nature. For some children the quietness simply reflects a need to be alone and think about what's happened. They may not know what to say to you, and older children could be getting their talking needs met with friends. For some children the quietness may be their way of trying to get your attention. If they're normally a lively, outgoing child, then their silence may be a call for help. If other members of the family have used silence as a weapon in the past, then a child refusing to talk may be a way of demonstrating anger and punishing parents.

Nigel says: 'Consider how your child has reacted to difficult situations in the past, as this may give you some clues to their current response. Keep a balance between letting your children know you are available to them and respecting their need for privacy. It is often hard for children to name their feelings so be patient. Some children prefer to talk with others, extended family or friends. This may relate to a fear of upsetting you. Trying to get children to talk "face-to-face" can sometimes be hard, so use those opportunities when you are sitting next to each other doing something else. It can feel less confrontational. Be patient.'

THE ANGRY CHILD

Children of all ages may react with anger. Their anger may be very obvious, with shouting and abusiveness, or it may be much more subtle, with moodiness and slamming doors.

Outer structure can help to ease the inner turmoil.

Toddlers to teenagers may refuse to do what they're told and become rude and cheeky. Their logic may be: 'You're not doing what I want, so why should I do what you want?' As mentioned in Chapter 4, children have a very strong sense of justice and fairness, and may rebel against anything that smacks of 'one rule for you and one rule for me'. Therefore, statements such as 'we're a family, we have to pull together' or 'remember you're not the only one with feelings' are likely to create more tension, not less. A younger child's rebellion may also be a call for attention. At this stage of the divorce process, many parents are preoccupied with the practical and emotional things that are going on, and children may receive less attention than they need. Children quickly learn that the fastest way to be noticed is to be naughty.

One of the most painful things that any parent will hear from their child is 'I hate you.' Unfortunately, this is a common refrain from children of divorce and, of course, it stems from deep feelings of anger and frustration. For parents who have previously enjoyed a good relationship with their child, you can be confident that, with support and reassurance, those old feelings of closeness will return. However, if the relationship has always been poor then the divorce may have compounded an existing problem. As well as working through the separation issues, you may need to re-assess your previous parenting relationship and find ways to strengthen it. Separate parenting can give an excellent opportunity to adjust your parenting style and improve relationships.

Nigel says: 'Anger is a common response to this difficult situation, and may be a child's way of dealing with distress. Show them it's all right to tell you how they feel. Let them know that you will listen and that you are strong enough to hear it. It's fine to make some allowances for children, but they also need to know that there are still boundaries in place.'

THE CLINGY OR FRAGILE CHILD

A significant sense of insecurity is likely to hit most children soon after the news has been broken, and often this is acted out in clingy behaviour. Both younger and older children may not want to be separated from either parent. Some will become particularly attached to the departing parent, fearing that they'll suddenly disappear while they're not looking. Others will cling to the parent who's staying at home, feeling they're the last bedrock of security. This clinginess can feel particularly draining for parents as they struggle to deal with their own emotions and needs.

Similar to the clingy child is the fragile child. A child who has perhaps usually been fairly healthy, independent and self-reliant may begin to complain of a host of minor ailments from tummy bugs to headaches, or even hinting at something much more serious. They may become scared and nervous of doing anything new or alone, and/or start experiencing problems at school or in friendship groups. This behaviour often hides a deeper anxiety that they're not going to cope and a fear that their needs may be overlooked. Occasionally it's an unconscious attempt to get Mum and Dad to stick together in order to look after them.

Nigel says: 'Acknowledge their distress and reassure them that even if you are living apart, you still love and care for them. Give them your time and attention. Routines are important; keep up with their usual activities where possible. Try not to criticise the other parent or have angry scenes in front of them. Children often have mixed feelings about what may have happened and they need you to understand their feelings, which may be different from your own.'

THE PERFECT CHILD

Some children will respond to the anxiety of family breakdown by becoming 'perfect'. They may become charming, considerate, cheerful, affectionate, thoughtful, tidy, organised, helpful and hardworking. Of course, all children can be like this occasionally, but the perfect child will attempt to be like this *all* the time. There are two main reasons for this behaviour. The first is to try to make things better for the parents. If one or both parents are obviously distressed, then a child may work extremely hard to cheer them up. Alternatively a child may become perfect to try to alleviate their anxiety that the separation was in some way their fault. Or they may try to make home life so perfect that Mum and Dad will want to stay together after all.

Nigel says: 'Talk to them; let them know you are pleased with their efforts to help, but also that you are strong enough to cope. Don't rely on them for your support; even if they are older this is the time when they need you. Let them know the separation was not their fault; they may need to hear this more than once. They need to know that even though you are separated you are still their parent who loves and cares for them.'

THE OKAY CHILD

Of course, some children will seem to be okay. They may have some angry days, some clingy and fragile ones, and occasionally they may be tearful or withdrawn, or even volunteer to tidy up without being asked. But none of their behaviour leads you to think that they're struggling in any way. And of course, this may genuinely be the case. If they're very young and their security is well maintained, or they're older teens who've been expecting the break-up and are engrossed in their own lives, then the emotional impact may be minimal. However, in some cases, a child's 'okayness' is a mask to hide deeper fears and anxieties. Some children don't want to be a burden on their parents, whom they might perceive as having enough to cope with as it is. Others may, rightly or wrongly, be picking up on signals that 'it's not okay not to be okay'.

Nigel says: 'Children can become very sensitive to you and may find it difficult to express their feelings or views if they feel you are unable or unwilling to hear what they may want to say. Talk to them. You don't have to go into all the details of the separation, but they do need to know the facts about their future – for example, contact visits and where they will be living and attending school. How they see you coping will also give them strategies for coming to terms with their own position.'

Remember that you know your children best. You know what is normal behaviour for them and what isn't. All children will react differently – and that includes siblings in the same house. You may have one child who seems to be really obviously struggling while the other one just doesn't seem to know what all the fuss is about. Only you will know if this is typical of your children, or if one or both of them is reacting unusually.

Occasionally this kind of split behaviour within a family is indicative either of a conscious or unconscious collusion between the children. One may be acting more like Mum and the other more like Dad in order to try and maintain some kind of balance. If that's the case, then you both need to reassure them that it's okay for them to be themselves and express their feelings openly. Or it may be that one child is acting okay and letting the other child demonstrate all their negative emotions for them. They may feel that as long as one of them is being angry or sad, they don't need to. The problem is that this leaves one child feeling stuck in the role of showing all the emotions, and feeling stressed as a result, and the other child receiving little attention for their quieter concerns. If you think that this may be happening in your household, then sit down with each child and talk to them about how they're feeling individually (There are some suggestions for doing this at the end of Chapter 6.) Encourage them to support each other, but also make sure they know that they're each entitled to show all the feelings that they have. It's okay to be angry and sad, and it's also okay to be fine on some days.

From the casebook

Gemma was fourteen, Alex was twelve and Sophie was nine when they came to Relate family counselling with their mum. Gemma said that she was fine about the divorce. She knew things were bad because she'd overheard lots of rows, and anyway she had her friends, who were all really lovely and supportive. Mum described Sophie as a little angel. She was coping really well and had started doing lots of chores around the house to help Mummy. Sophie said that she liked helping Mummy and it wasn't fair that Mummy had to do everything on her own now that Daddy had gone. Alex was sullen and angry. He didn't want to come for family counselling and was very reluctant to engage at all. He hated his mum, hated his sisters, hated his school and hated his life. He wanted to live with Dad and said that until Mum let him, he would continue to be disruptive and abusive. At times his behaviour had been violent. Over the coming weeks it became apparent that Alex felt that nobody cared about Dad any more. He said that the girls had both taken Mum's side and someone had to stick up for Dad. Nobody was being angry with Mum for making the decision to separate, and he felt that someone had to do that. We spent time as a family talking about what each member felt and as each heard the other saying that they also felt angry sometimes, Alex felt able to let go of the responsibility of being 'the angry one'. As his behaviour changed at home, so did Sophie's. She no longer felt she had to defend Mum by always being a good girl and began to get a bit angrier herself. It was difficult at first for everyone to adjust to playing different roles, but all agreed that it felt fairer on everyone and no one felt left out any more.

HELP FROM OTHERS

Children can benefit from the help and support of a number of different people during this difficult time. There may be some people, such as grandparents or family friends, to whom they've always been close. There may also be others that you haven't thought about – parents of their friends, teachers, youth group or activity leaders. Have a think about the kind of activities they're involved in and, in particular, the adults they've talked about in the past. Who have they said they like or thought was 'really nice'? Could you talk to these people about the situation? If your child is old enough, could he or she approach them directly? Of course, your child may not want to confide in anybody else, but if you think it may be helpful, talk to them about it and ask if there's anything you can do to make it easier for this to happen. In Chapter 3 we dealt with telling others; it's important also to remember that if these are people that are going to be able to support your child, both they and your child need to know that any conversations between the two of them will be confidential.

In some instances, a parent, child, teacher or friend may think that counselling would be helpful. You'll need to look in your area to find out what's available. Your GP should also be able to help you. Many schools recruit a counsellor, and most Relate centres have people who are specifically trained to work with children going through family change. Often just a few sessions are enough to give your child a safe place in which to explore and understand their feelings, though sometimes a child may want to continue for quite some time, particularly if there are ongoing changes within the home. Occasionally a counsellor or GP will suggest that you go for family counselling so that all of you can share what's going on and explore ways to make things better.

Children can also find it helpful to explore their feelings through books or information on the Internet. Depending on the age of the child, you might want to do this together or leave them to do it alone. There's a comprehensive list of Resources at the back of this book to help with this.

TALKING AND LISTENING TO YOUR CHILDREN

Children of all ages feel loved and valued when we listen to them. When we consciously make regular time to listen to our children and give them our full attention, we learn to understand how they are feeling, and it lets them know that they're important.

We can help children to talk by:
➤ Giving them 100 per cent of your attention.
➤ Minimise any distractions (for example, turn off the television and don't answer the phone).
➤ Let them speak in their own time and express their feelings.
➤ Feed back what you think your child is feeling. For example, 'It sounds as if you're feeling angry. Is that right?'
➤ Listen to your child without judgement or criticism.
➤ Interrupt only to clarify what your child has said.
➤ Give them as much time as they need and let them stop when they want to.
➤ If your child wants to play or move about, let them, and follow at a distance while you continue to listen.
➤ Summarise and feed back to your child your understanding of what he or she has said.
➤ Tell them that you're glad that they've spoken to you, even though it may have been difficult.

CHAPTER 6

Agreeing New Living Arrangements

With two out of every five marriages ending in divorce there are now an estimated 3 million children in the UK living in a separated household. An average of 150,000 children experience their parents divorce each year. In addition, it is estimated that an equal number of children of co-habiting parents see their parents separate, making a total of approximately 300,000 children living in separated families. And every one of those households does it differently. Some will have come up with a workable solution almost immediately, while others have reached an adequate compromise through trial and error.

When trying to decide what arrangements will work for you, your priority should be thinking about what your children will need. Experts agree that, wherever possible, it's best to maintain as much of the status quo as you can. (See Chapter 8 for advice about establishing routines.)

Other things you need to consider are the financial and geographic practicalities. Wherever possible, your children should continue to have the usual access to friends and extended family members, and the same routines regarding school and activities. And of course, your financial situation will play a critical role. If it's feasible, it's best for children to be able to stay within the same family home to minimise the degree of change to which they have to adapt – but sometimes it's just not possible.

In the vast majority of cases, parents agree the new living arrangements between themselves without any legal intervention. A survey by the Office of National Statistics found that around one in ten parents had court orders. Between half and 60 per cent agreed contact between themselves, and between 20 per cent and 35 per cent had no formal arrangements. If you can't agree, then you may need to seek advice either through mediation or the legal system – there's more about this in Chapter 12. But ideally you'll be able to agree things between yourselves.

The more you can agree as a couple, the easier it will be to maintain flexibility and change plans as your children's needs grow. It also demonstrates to your children that you're still able to co-operate with each other in their best interests. Of course, this can feel extremely difficult. As we've already seen in Chapters 1 and 2, emotions can run very high at this time, and both of you are almost certainly going to want to do as much as you possibly can to maintain a good, regular relationship with your children. However, it is often the fear of not seeing the children that fuels residency and contact arguments. Remember that both of you love your children and want only what is best for them. Read Chapter 9 to discover how you and your partner can try to address some of these difficult negotiations with minimal conflict.

There are some incidents where regular contact with a parent would not be safe for children – for example, where there is violence, abuse or significant neglect. If this applies to you then you'll find more about this in Chapters 11 and 12.

What follows is a summary of some of the most common options for living arrangements, and some thoughts and comments from Resolution, the organisation of family solicitors, which promotes resolving disputes in a non-confrontational manner.

SHARED RESIDENCE – ONE HOME

This option allows the children to continue to live in the same house and have regular live-in contact with both Mum and Dad alternately. Typically, each parent will have homes elsewhere and move into the family home for a few days at a time. For example, Mum might live there from Monday to Thursday then go to her other home, and Dad would move in from Friday to Sunday. This has the advantage of the kids not having to move, as well as having maximum contact with parents. However, it's disruptive to parents, potentially means having three homes, or parents sharing the same flat when not in the family home, and is difficult to maintain if/when a new partner is introduced. If parents have different rules, it's also very confusing for kids to be allowed food in their bedroom one night but not the next.

Resolution says: 'In practice this arrangement works best when (a) there is a lot of available money to provide for three homes and (b) the parents have an excellent relationship as co-parents. This arrangement usually works in the initial time of separation before the divorce and financial settlement. It is a pattern which rarely emerges as a long-term arrangement.'

SHARED RESIDENCE – TWO HOMES

As above, children get regular live-in contact with both parents but they move between two households. Assuming the households are reasonably close together, children can continue at the same school and see the same friends. Time may be split each week or alternate weeks, though it doesn't necessarily have to be split equally.

When trying to decide what arrangements will work for you, your priority should be thinking about what your children will need.

'I spend equal time with Mum and Dad, and I feel okay with that. I see Dad Monday and Tuesday nights, and then his partner takes me to school on Wednesday. Then Mum picks me up from school on Wednesdays and we go to her. At weekends, we take turns with Mum and Dad. I think all that will continue even if it changes slightly. They always check it out with us. I feel it's up to me. Like I did say I wanted to spend more time with Dad because I didn't think I was spending enough time with him. And they sorted something out. Sometimes they have little meetings and in these meetings they talk about what we want. Then they work out what they have to do.'
Gabriella, aged eight

For example, some families choose to let the children live with Dad every weekend, but Monday to Friday with Mum. In the latter arrangement, geography is less important. Many children like this arrangement, at least at first, but it can become very tiring, and some say they feel as though they can't properly settle in either home and are constantly living out of a suitcase.

Resolution says: 'This is becoming the "typical" arrangement, as more and more fathers demonstrate their ability to take an equal role in day-to-day parenting tasks. It is one that is increasingly ordered by the courts. Like all contact plans it works best when the parents can co-operate with each other and are flexible over precise arrangements. Where possible, a duplicate set of clothes and equipment at both homes is important to help minimise the "suitcase kid" syndrome.'

SOLE RESIDENCE WITH AGREED CONTACT

This is probably the most common scenario, especially with younger children. If finances allow, the children stay in the family home living with one parent – usually Mum. Contact is agreed with Dad on a regular basis so everyone knows that the kids are at Dad's, for example, on Tuesday evenings and alternate weekends. In this scenario there is minimal disruption to the children's day-to-day living arrangements, but they lose a lot of access to one parent. Sometimes, financial pressures mean that the family home can't be maintained, and the children move to a smaller house with Mum or Dad.

Resolution says: 'For many years this arrangement was the default arrangement and considered "reasonable" by courts and mothers. Defined contact can have advantages (everyone knows where they are) but some real disadvantages if the parents can't work together well – then the contact order becomes a stick with which to beat the other parent, leading to greater discord. This pattern also led to the sense in some mothers that contact was in their gift. It is not all negative, though. Where parents live geographically distant, this pattern is still the one that works best, particularly if parents are understanding about journey times and distances.'

> *'I stay every weekend at Dad's, the Saturday and Sunday. I used to go about nine in the morning but now I go skating on Saturday, so it depends on what time we finish there. If we lived very near him, I'd go and see him whenever, all the time. But we moved here. When I'm older, get to seventeen or something, I'll just go and see him during the week as well. When I've left school I will go and see him more often, spend more time with him. Definitely.'*
> *Chaz, aged fourteen*

SOLE RESIDENCE WITH AD HOC CONTACT

This is similar to the above arrangement, but the parents don't formalise any contact arrangements. This often works best for older children who like to choose for themselves how much time they spend with the non-resident parent. While it offers maximum flexibility for children, some forward planning is generally required to ensure everyone knows what's going on.

Resolution says: 'The majority of separating families probably adopt this pattern. It allows fluidity/ flexibility and, to a large extent, can best reflect the needs of individual children rather than "the children" as a package.'

'My sister and I live with Mum, but see Dad whenever we want to. He lives in a flat just round the corner, so sometimes we can just pop in after school or we can go for a whole evening or stay the night. He took us on holiday for a week in the summer, which was really good. We can arrange things whenever we want to. We text or phone or whatever. Neither of them seems to mind as long as we give them some notice so they know whether or not we're having tea there. We're getting better at having things in both places but there's always something you forget and if it's something important for school it's a real pain. I don't think Mum or Dad realise how much of a pain it is.'
Charlotte, aged fifteen

CONTINUING TOGETHER IN THE SAME HOME

Some couples whose separation has been reasonably amicable may decide to separate, but continue to live in the same house. They may tell the children that they've separated, and 'legally' separate, but they maintain the same shared home. This has obvious advantages of minimum disruption to the children's daily lives, but can be awkward and confusing. Younger children may not understand what's going on and assume that things are okay, or maintain the fantasy that Mum and Dad will get back together. Older children can feel it's a farce and prefer a clean break.

Resolution says: 'This is a short-term solution requiring a high degree of co-operation between the parents. It will be short-term because life moves on, one or other parent may want to re-partner, and this cannot easily be accommodated when everyone is under one roof! It is a pattern more likely to work when the children are older or more mature, as it might lead to confusion amongst younger or immature children. If it is to work for younger children, parents need to give very clear, unambiguous joint messages to them about the reality. These messages can be reinforced by the parents agreeing designated days to be responsible for childcare (as if they were physically separated) and by keeping the number of joint activities to a minimum.'

> *Whatever you decide, remember the two things that matter most to your children are: seeing each of their parents as much as possible; and maintaining as many regular routines as possible.*

MOVING IN WITH A NEW PARTNER

A number of couples split up because one of them has met a new partner and has moved in with him or her. They may be in love and sure that this is what they want to do, but it's often the worst scenario for children – especially if they want the children to live with them. There are already so many things for a child to adjust to, and having to adapt to a significant new person in their parent's life can feel totally overwhelming. They're also much more likely to feel resentful of this new person and blame them for the breakdown of their parents' relationship. As you'll see in the following chapters, the first few weeks and months are the toughest for everyone involved, and the more you can do to reduce the stress the better. If at all possible, it's best to live alone at first and then introduce a new partner at a later date when the news of the break-up has begun to sink in and

'Mum left Dad five years ago to live with Tom. I was nine. I was too little then to really understand what was going on but I really didn't like Tom. As the years have gone on I've hated him more and more. If it wasn't for him, Mum wouldn't have left. Dad's told me that their relationship wouldn't have worked anyway, but I still hate the fact that she had an affair. I'll never forgive her for what she did. She broke up our family because she loved Tom more than any of us. My sister feels the same as me. She hates him as well. She tries to make out that she's okay with it but she tells me all the time that she's not. And I hear Mum and Tom arguing all the time. It's not even like it's going to work out.'
Jack, aged fourteen

everyone is beginning to settle. This is also likely to minimise negative consequences that you and your new partner may have to live with for many years to come. There's more on introducing a new partner in Chapter 11.

Resolution says: 'Introducing a new partner can often cause major difficulties for families both in terms of the effect on the children but also in terms of the relationship as co-parent with your former partner. The former partner can often feel marginalised and frightened of having their parental role usurped. It is important not to dismiss these feelings. They often have a knock-on effect on the children, as they can feel a loyalty to their absent parent which disrupts their ability to form a new relationship with the new partner. There are often tensions between the old and new partners which spill out into the whole family. Great care must be taken in introducing a new partner – both the fact of their existence and the first meeting between them and the children. Moving in with them should be a step taken only when the children are comfortable with the new partner and once it is clear to all concerned how the new partner fits into the parenting hierarchy.'

As you can see, there is no perfect solution. Whatever you decide will be a compromise. When making your decision you need to think about the particular requirements of your children and what fits best with your individual circumstances. Remember also that you'll need to be flexible. What you agree now might need to change in the future – perhaps because working patterns change or because the children decide that they would like a new system as they grow older.

It's important that children feel included in the decisions that are being made. Older children in particular will expect to have a say in the way their lives are to be managed. But even quite young children respond well to feeling they have some choices in the way things are set up. Children of different ages may need different agreements. An ad hoc arrangement may work very well for teenage children but younger siblings may feel more reassured if there's a fixed routine. Many parents find it difficult to consider different arrangements for siblings, thinking that the children 'should be kept together'. However, there is no evidence to suggest that this is better for children. On the contrary, many children say they prefer it when they have the chance to spend time alone with each parent.

Whatever you decide, remember the two things that matter most to your children are: seeing each of their parents as much as possible; and maintaining as many regular routines as possible.

You'll also need to consider how you'll split the household contents in a way that is fair for each of you, but also for the children. They will need to feel at home, wherever they happen to be staying. Therefore they'll need some of their own things around them and also some familiar items from home. There's more on this in Chapter 7.

Your finances will be another very important issue to consider. If you're selling a property, how will you split the equity? If you're not, what will happen to any equity in the house? These issues are best discussed with a solicitor, and you'll find more details on this in Chapter 12.

PRESERVING RELATIONSHIPS WHEREVER YOU LIVE

Home is much, much more than a house. Home is where you can feel relaxed and be yourself. At the end of the day, it's the relationship you have with your children that matters. It is your relationship that they'll remember for the rest of their life, not the bricks and mortar of a building. Whatever arrangement you end up with is simply the framework for your relationship as a parent. If it's not ideal, which undoubtedly it won't be, focus both your and your children's attention on the advantages of the situation and on the quality of the relationship they're going to continue to have with you.

I'll leave the final word in this chapter to the Department of Social Policy and Social Work at the University of Oxford, which said in a family policy briefing document:

'It is not the arrangements in themselves which matter most to children but how their relationships are managed. Children may vary in their responses to the same arrangements even within the same family. However, flexibility and the ability to accommodate other parts of their lives, such as social activities, may be particularly important to older children; frequency and regularity for younger ones. Children who are consulted about decisions and are able to talk to a parent about problems are more likely to feel positive about arrangements.'

The following list of questions can help you to consider the many needs of your children when thinking about future living arrangements. Many of the points are covered in more depth in Chapter 8:

➤ What are our financial commitments and restrictions?
➤ How do our working patterns impact on seeing the children and caring for them?
➤ What other adults could/should they see regularly?
➤ Will the children have maximum access to each parent?
➤ How often will the children see each parent?
➤ Will your arrangements be formally fixed, or ad hoc?
➤ How will you split school holidays?
➤ How will you organise celebration days such as birthdays and Christmas?
➤ How close will parents live to each other?
➤ How will moving between households be managed?
➤ How will you split household contents?
➤ Where will pets live?
➤ Will children still be close to friends and extended family members?
➤ Will all out-of-school activities be maintained and who will take them?
➤ What will you do about attending parents' evenings, sports days, school events, football matches?
➤ How can children keep in contact with the other parent when not staying with them?
➤ How can children keep in touch with extended family when with the other parent?

CHAPTER 7

Managing Leaving Day

The day one of you leaves the family home is a day that you will remember for many years to come – and your children will probably remember for ever. It's a day that is often not only busy with the hustle and bustle of moving but also full of mixed emotions for everyone. For parents there are often powerful feelings of sadness and loss, as well as some feelings of relief. For children there is also a lot of sadness, but often also the excitement of a new home to visit or stay in. For everyone it is the day when the separation is now very, very real, and even if you've had many weeks or even months leading up to it, the actual reality of the physical separation is often profound.

There is no way of avoiding the practical and emotional impact of departure day, but thorough preparation can help you minimise the effects. The more that children can be involved in the practicalities of moving out, the easier it will be for them to see the day as a beginning of a new phase of their family life, rather than the end of it.

PREPARING FOR LEAVING DAY

Ideally you will have already told the children some weeks or days ago (see Chapter 3) so they will be aware of what's going on. But even if you've said it before, once the actual date has been agreed it's worth going through the basics again, particularly for younger children, who may have forgotten. If the departure is very sudden, or has already happened, then there is some specific guidance for you later in this chapter.

Before you can agree a date, the departing parent needs to find somewhere to live. It can be beneficial for children of all ages to be included in the house-hunting process. Not only because they may also live there for some of the time, but more importantly because it affirms they will continue to be part of the leaving parent's life. If you're not buying or renting another home but living with someone else, either temporarily or permanently, the children can be encouraged to visit the new house and see the parent's room and also any rooms where they will visit or stay. They might help to decorate or rearrange furniture and decide where things will go.

Even if children aren't going to visit the new home regularly, it's important that they can visualise where the other parent will be. Remember that children often worry about the welfare of their parents after a separation, and some, especially young children, may fantasise about all sorts of horrors. Seeing where the parent will live can allay a host of fears and anxieties that the children themselves may not have consciously known that they had.

It's important that the sadness and pain of the separation are not denied or minimised, so that a child feels unable to express their feelings of sadness, but it's equally as important for children to feel confident that there is life ahead.

Children can also be involved in buying things for the new home – including items for their own room as well as general household bits and pieces. If this kind of activity can be undertaken with an appropriate degree of casualness by each parent, then this can further reinforce the message that things are going to be okay. As mentioned before, it's important that the sadness and pain of the separation are not denied or minimised, so that a child feels unable to express their feelings of sadness, but it's equally important for children to feel confident that there is life ahead.

Some children may not want to be involved in helping a parent move out in any way. It may be too painful for them. They may feel angry at the departing parent, or think that 'helping' may be seen as condoning what has happened. If this is the case then respect their decision not to be involved, but continue to keep them informed and encourage them to take part in any way they want to.

It's also good to involve children in planning the actual departure day itself. As a general rule, it's best if it's early in the day so that no one is hanging around feeling apprehensive. Also, make sure it's a day when everyone is available and nothing significant is going on. Obviously that means avoiding birthdays or other anniversaries, but also try to avoid a time close to an activity that's significant for a child, such as an important sports tournament or performance. It's also best, if you can, to do the whole move in one day. When a parent keeps returning to remove more and more things from the home, children can feel very unsettled and worry that one day there'll be nothing left.

Ideally you should agree as a couple how you'll manage the practicalities of the day. If you're the partner who's staying, will you help pack or will you keep busy in another room? Will you wave goodbye to each other? Will you hand over keys? There are no right or wrong answers to these questions; they are simply the awkward formalities that you need to agree – preferably beforehand. Some people find it helps to have other people around to dilute the tension. Maybe a grandparent to provide support, or a close friend to help shift furniture. If you do decide to have other people there, make sure they're people that are close to the children, rather than strangers who may make them feel nervous.

Children can be included in deciding what they would like to do on the day. Do they want to help pack? Do they want to go with the departing parent and set up the new house, or stay behind and re-shuffle the old house? Again, there's no right or wrong, and siblings may decide they want to do different things. Some children, particularly older ones, might prefer not to be around at all and instead spend the day with friends. That's okay, but make sure they're aware of how different the house will be when they return so they're not too shocked.

Wherever the children choose to spend the day, that first evening is going to feel very different. If they're going to stay at home then normal routines will probably be out of the window anyway, but maybe that's okay just for this one day. Be prepared to do something different: get a takeaway, eat in front of the TV, or go out and perhaps spend time with close family friends. Small children may want to spend the night in your room or with an older sibling. It's fine to make exceptions during this very stressful time, but, as previously mentioned, it's also important to re-establish the stability of routines as soon as possible.

> *'I remember the day Mum left like it was yesterday. Dad was screaming at her and she was crying. I'll never forget it.'*
> *Alice, aged fourteen (six years after her parents split up)*

WHEN THE DEPARTURE IS/WAS SUDDEN

If your partner has already gone, or has just announced that they're going tomorrow or at the weekend, then you have little or no time to prepare either yourself or your children. Like many people in your situation, you may need extra help from friends and family to cope at this very difficult time, so that you can still find the strength to support your children. You'll probably need to work particularly hard at putting any feelings of shock, anger and bewilderment to one side while you reassure your children that things are going to be okay. Even if you're not sure yourself how you're going to cope, your children need to know that, one way or another, you will.

If at all possible, try to contact your ex, and agree a time when you can meet to discuss your children's needs. As well as establishing the new living arrangements, hopefully you can also agree a time when the two of you can talk to your children about the future. If this isn't possible, then all you can do is once again reassure your children that even though things have changed, you're still a family and you both still love them. Say that you don't exactly know what's going to happen but you're going to be right by their side and you'll let them know as soon as you can.

> *'I'd like to tell her how special she is to me.'*
> *Billy, aged nine (talking about her mum after her dad had left)*

SPLITTING THE HOUSEHOLD POSSESSIONS

One of the worst tasks of splitting up is dividing up the household possessions. Not only can this be a complicated task practically – Who should have the drill? Who's going to use it most? Who's got space to store it? Can one of you take it and the other borrow it if need be? – but it also evokes a lot of emotions. Some things may be quite straightforward – presents from other people to just one of you, an inherited family heirloom, or something you had yourself as a child – while other things are much more difficult, such as wedding presents, things you chose together for your home, or holiday souvenirs.

Children need to have familiar things around them to help them feel secure. This means that the home where the children will spend most of their time will ideally have more familiar things in it, and the house that is occasionally visited can just have some essential items plus things that the children would like to be there, too. Your first priority should be deciding what needs to stay or go for the children's sake. Once you've done that, you can then begin to allocate the non-essential items.

The system that seems to work best for people is to start by splitting all the non-contentious items and leave the difficult things till last. Begin with the easy stuff, and take it in turns to choose the items that you want. When you get down to the difficult items, hopefully the turn-taking system can still work. So, for example, you may have each taken the CDs that you want and you are left with a pile of eight that you both would like. Flip a coin for who goes first and then take it in turns till all eight have gone.

Some children will get quite upset at the thought, or the sight, of things being removed. It can feel as if their home is being dismantled, bit by bit.

Of course a CD can be replaced, but souvenirs and other items of sentimental value cannot. If you can, try to trade: 'Maybe I could have the picture over the fireplace and you could have the lamp.' Ultimately some things will be very difficult, but remember that if they are family heirlooms, one way or another, they'll probably end up being passed down to your children anyway. Fortunately photos are less difficult than they used to be, as most can be copied.

If there is still a lot of anger or sadness about the separation, emotions may run particularly high. If a partner decides they don't want to take something, it can feel like a further rejection. Equally, when your ex insists on taking something you value, it can feel as if they're rubbing salt into the wound. Some people will offer to walk away with nothing because their guilt tells them they have no right to anything any more. Someone else might refuse to let a partner take anything, as their anger tells them that this is justified punishment for what they've done. It is rarely the possessions themselves that couples are actually fighting over, but what they represent.

While you and your ex are deciding what belongs to whom, your children will tend to see almost everything as belonging to them. It's in their house and it may have been there ever since they were born, therefore it's 'theirs'. Some children will get quite upset at the thought, or the sight, of things being removed. It can feel as if their home is being dismantled, bit by bit. Be sure to reassure children that the things they treasure are still staying in your family but just moving to a new house, and that they will still see them. You can also minimise the stress by filling up the gaps quickly with other items or by shuffling things around.

Both of you, whether you're the one leaving or staying, will have the task of creating – or rather, recreating – a home for your children. Somewhere they can feel safe and secure and loved. Though it can be painful dividing the possessions, remember that your goal should continue to be what is best for your children, and try to put your own feelings to one side.

YOUR FEELINGS IF YOU'RE THE ONE LEAVING

Whether or not the decision was yours to leave, you will have to adjust the most. Not only are you leaving your partner, but you are also leaving your home and day-to-day contact with your children. If you didn't want the relationship to end, then departure day may be particularly painful for you. Mixed with the sadness may be anger at having to leave so much behind against your will. But even if you chose to leave, you're still likely to feel the pain of loss and perhaps anger at your partner, yourself, or just life in general that it all had to come to this.

'I just couldn't believe how much I missed him.'
Ben, aged fourteen

The most painful loss for many is the loss of daily contact with children. Your new home may seem very quiet compared to the hustle and bustle of family life. Without the near-constant demands that children of any age seem to impose on their parents, your new environment may feel empty and lifeless.

You may also feel fear and anxiety about the future. Even if you'd spent time thinking about how things would be once you'd left, it's still common to worry about how you'll cope alone once you finally find that you are. During the early days it's typical for a lot of old feelings to resurface. You may have thought you'd already worked through your feelings of anger, sadness, fear, doubt or guilt, but the reality of separation often brings them back. If this applies to you, then you may find that reading or re-reading Chapter 2 will help you to understand what you're going through.

Even if you're not sure yourself how you're going to cope, your children need to know that, one way or another, you will.

But as well as the negative emotions, many departing partners will also feel a sense of relief. Now you're no longer living in the tension of a house in transition, you can begin to think about how you want your future to be.

YOUR FEELINGS IF YOU'RE THE ONE STAYING

If your partner has left you against your wishes then you may suddenly find yourself swamped with feelings of abandonment and loneliness. Even if you've prepared yourself for leaving day, you may be shocked at how powerful the feelings are. If you were the one who initiated the ending, then you may feel relief that you can now move on with your life, but don't be surprised if you also feel lonely and have pangs of longing for your ex. Old feelings that you'd thought you'd dealt with often resurface once the separation has become real. Reassure yourself that this is normal, and give yourself space and permission to grieve. There's more help in Chapter 2.

The parent who stays in the family home usually has to cope with the bulk of the children's emotional needs. Even if you've agreed joint residency, children will be more likely to express their negative feelings in the comfort of familiar surroundings then they will in the new house. This can also trigger intense feelings of anger at a partner who chose to leave, or guilt if you were the one who decided to end it. Many parents can feel overwhelmed by the responsibilities of running the family home alone, and it's common to experience intense feelings of anxiety.

> **'Mum just fell apart for the first week – it was awful.'**
> **Lewis, aged eleven**

Whether or not you chose to end the relationship, most people also feel relief. Living with a partner who is on the verge of leaving is incredibly stressful, and turning that final corner, however painful, can feel like a positive step. You can also reclaim your home as your own, and many people enjoy changing the niggling things that have annoyed them for years. I remember a thirty-eight-year-old man, whose wife had left him suddenly after fifteen years, proudly announcing that he had moved all the mirrors in the house up eight inches. Being much taller than her had meant he'd spent fifteen years stooping every time he'd wanted to look in a mirror!

HELPING THE CHILDREN COPE

The first few weeks after leaving are probably the toughest for everyone. An empty space at the dining table or in front of the television. Only one person to play with or to read the bedtime story. And if you're the parent who's alone, then you may find yourself with time on your hands and remembering how things used to be. For all of you, it's a time of significant adjustment.

As we said earlier, it's common for parents to experience powerful emotions at this time, and, of course, this is equally true of children. And in the same way as old feelings may resurface for parents, they may also resurface for children. Many of the questions you've already answered may be asked again, and you may be confronted anew with their anger and sadness. You may also experience further changes in children's behaviour, or regression to behaviour of a younger age. This is perfectly normal and needs to be handled with sensitivity and firmness. Your children need your support now, perhaps more than at any other time in the divorce process. Unfortunately, now may also be the time you feel least able to give it.

Extremes of emotion can be frightening and unsettling for children. If they can't see that you're coping, how can they begin to imagine that they'll be able to?

Make sure that you get support for yourself from friends, family or professionals so you have somewhere to share the extremes of your emotions rather than letting your children see them. That doesn't mean that you have to shut yourself away every time you want to cry, as it's important that children see that this is a painful time and that it's okay to be sad and angry. But extremes of emotion can be frightening and unsettling for children. And if they can't see that you're coping, how can they begin to imagine that they'll be able to?

However you feel, remember that your parental responsibilities have not changed. You are still responsible for the welfare of your children. For ensuring that they still have good, regular contact with you and a solid relationship with their other parent. At this time when angry feelings can resurface with a vengeance, it's more essential than ever that you don't blame your partner or put them down in front of the children. Your views and feelings towards your ex-partner are not relevant to how your children relate to them as a parent. What's more, many children will take negative comments about a parent very personally and will feel as if you're putting down a piece of *them*.

Whatever you're feeling, you need to be positive about the

new arrangements and show a determination to accept this new phase of family life. It's fine to tell them that you miss them and that you're sad, but make sure this is balanced with reassurance that you're still close to them when you're apart and that your relationship doesn't need to suffer. You can also show a positive attitude towards the future by getting both houses organised and resettled as quickly as possible. Reinstate or continue routines, and show that, so far as family is concerned, it's business as usual. Always remember that change is stressful for children, so don't be tempted to make too many household changes such as decorating or moving rooms around until a later date.

> *'After Mum put us to bed, my sister would climb into my bed and we'd go to sleep. We never talked, just cuddled.'*
> *Samina and Kajit, aged seven and nine*

Below is a checklist to help you and your ex settle your children into the new family regimes as soon as possible:

➤ Get both houses organised as soon as possible so children can feel at home.

➤ Encourage contact with the absent parent as early as possible and establish contact routines.

➤ Make sure children know where each of you is during the day, and that you're contactable if necessary.

➤ Don't make any major decisions or significant changes till the dust settles.

➤ Protect your children from extremes of emotion, but do let them know that you're sad, too.

➤ Make sure they know it's okay to show their feelings.

➤ Continue to tell them you both love them.

➤ Continue to reassure them that it's not their fault.

➤ Be ready to answer the why questions again.

➤ Don't say negative things about the absent parent.

➤ Make sure your child knows you want them to see the other parent.

CHAPTER 8

Establishing and Maintaining New Routines

Once the dust of leaving day has settled it's time to get on with the rest of your life. For some, this will be a huge relief. A painful relationship is now in the past and a new future lies ahead. It's a second chance to find a more mutually fulfilling relationship. For others the future may be looking bleak. Whatever your view, the one thing that has not changed is the fact that you're a mum or a dad. You may no longer be partners, but you are both still parents.

As well as continuing to get support for yourself, you need to establish good contact regimes for your children. Assuming there are no safety reasons for your children not to see your ex (see Chapter 11), then you should be encouraging as much contact as possible. And by contact, I mean telephone, email and text, as well as direct face-to-face time. Research shows that children cope best with divorce when they continue to have regular contact with both parents. And more important than frequency of contact is the quality of it. Most children would prefer to have a few hours of their parents' full, undivided attention than a whole day of watching TV alone while their parent is in another room working on the computer.

SETTING UP GOOD CONTACT REGIMES

The specific details of your contact arrangements will depend on the ages of your children and on your individual circumstances. Hopefully you and your partner will have already agreed – either formally through the courts or informally as most couples do – the amount and regularity of contact. Now is the time to put those plans into action. On paper, contact arrangements can seem quite straightforward, but in reality some things don't work out quite as well as you'd imagined. One father, who lives twenty miles from the family home, has the kids on alternate Saturdays, and has to do a forty-mile round trip for his son's football in the morning then the same again for his daughter's ballet. It's not that he minds the driving, but the children complain that they spend most of the day in the car.

You may no longer be partners, but you are both still parents.

It's essential to stay as flexible about arrangements as you can and to keep listening to the children's views. This is particularly important if a parent has to travel with work and sometimes misses agreed contact times. But that doesn't mean you should be constantly changing plans. On the contrary, it's equally as important for a child's sense of stability to stick to agreed days and times as much as is humanly possible. This is particularly important for the non-resident parent. Being continually late or cancelling arrangements tells a child that they're not as important as something else. No matter how good your reasons may be, to a child, going back on what you've agreed is breaking a promise, and will, almost always, be taken as a personal rejection.

'Mum's let me down too many times – I don't want to give her another chance.' Joshua, aged ten

In the early months, make sure you constantly reinforce the message to children that you want a relationship with them and nothing will get in the way of that.

As well as regular face-to-face contact, remember to keep in touch as often as possible via phone, text messaging, email and/or instant chat. This is something that's best agreed between parents as it can sometimes feel like an intrusion if one parent is constantly texting or phoning during the other parent's time. In addition to the regular contact you agree, let children know they can contact the other parent whenever they want to.

HANDOVER TIMES

The handover of children can often be a source of tension for parents, especially in the first year when emotions can still be raw. It's important that children are as protected as possible from the pain that can be around at handover time. Therefore, tough as it may be, smile when your ex comes to collect them or when you drop them off, and give them a cheery wave goodbye. Remember that your children need to see that it's okay for them to leave you and see the other parent.

From the casebook
Molly and Kate, aged eleven and nine, came to me for family counselling when Kate's behaviour at school was deteriorating. Their parents had split up eight months ago, and Molly described how Mum cried every time they went to see Dad. Mum had never wanted the divorce and was open about how much she missed Dad. She would leave the room in tears if he rang the girls, or if she heard the beep of a text message. Molly was able to verbalise how this made her feel torn between her parents, but Kate, being younger, found it harder to express her mixed emotions and instead was acting up at school. Mum was very upset when she heard what impact her sadness was having on her daughters. She resolved to get some counselling for herself, ask for more support from friends, and proactively encourage the girls to see their dad.

If the pain of seeing an ex really is too great to bear, or if arguments seem to be impossible to avoid, then you could consider arranging things so that the children are collected directly from school or from a familiar other home such as a grandparent's or a family friend's.

As a general rule, you should avoid using handover times for any kind of discussion about the children or other arrangements – especially if there's a chance that there will be disagreements. Any conversations that you need to have about practicalities can be done over the phone, via email or in a separate face-to-face meeting – basically, any time that is separate from the children's time with the other parent. You can make handovers even smoother by ensuring the children are ready to leave and have everything with them that they will want or need to take to the other house.

TRANSITIONAL ANXIETY

Psychologists have coined the term 'transitional anxiety' to describe how many children often behave around the time of handovers. Before leaving to go to the other parent, it's common for a child to become quiet or withdrawn, or to play up. This is because they are feeling the pain of the coming separation from one parent mixed with excited or anxious anticipation of seeing the other parent. Many children feel nervous about split loyalties. If they show too much enthusiasm about seeing the other parent, will the present parent feel upset or angry? Some verbalise negative thoughts about the pending visit in order to make a parent feel better, even though they know they'll have a great time when they get there. They may also go to great lengths to say how much they'll miss the parent they're leaving behind.

Children can also react badly when they return from a visit

to the non-resident parent. They may be upset, clingy, angry, aggressive and uncooperative. Again, this is a very common reaction as a child takes time to adjust. They'll almost certainly be missing the other parent, and may temporarily feel disorientated. Experts think that it takes between six to twelve months for children to get used to contact arrangements, and the best thing you can do during this time is maintain routines and stability, and accept that this is normal behaviour. It would be easy to think that the behaviour is an indication the child isn't enjoying contact, but this is almost never the case. Even the child who openly says that they haven't enjoyed a visit is often only saying this to confirm their allegiance with the resident parent. If you think your child genuinely doesn't want to see their other parent, then there's more on this in Chapter 9.

You can also help your child simply by telling them you realise how hard this all is for them. For example, saying, 'I know it's tough saying goodbye to one of us and hello to the other – but it will get easier over time,' can really help a child to feel less alone in their struggle.

VISITS WITH THE NON-RESIDENT PARENT

If you're the non-resident parent, remember that spending time with you is going to feel very strange to your child at first. Because they're almost certainly going to be in different surroundings. If they come to your new home, then try to engage them in an activity or share a meal with them as soon as they arrive to help them to settle. Consider having some special toys or activities that are only at your house – a Gameboy, Sky TV or a basketball hoop, for example.

If you're having to travel a long distance and spend a lot of your contact time out and about, make sure you've thought ahead about what you can do. Find places to visit, and always have a wet weather option up your sleeve.

Teenagers can often feel bored at the non-resident parent's house and may need extra persuasion to visit. This isn't personal; it's about being in a strange environment without their things around them. If you've left contact arrangements completely up to them, as many parents of older children do – an open door, 'you're welcome any time' policy – then it can be difficult for children to make the decision to visit. Try to create an informal structure for them that fits with the other demands on their life. Maybe always popping in to watch *The Simpsons,* or coming round on Wednesdays with chemistry homework. And create unique parent/child times like a football match once a month or a bumper sleepover with their mates.

HOLIDAYS

All families have different expectations of holiday times. You may have been a family that saved up for an annual two-week long-haul; perhaps you spent holidays visiting relatives or lazing around the garden. However you've managed holidays previously is going to determine how you now negotiate them with two separate parents. The age of your children will also be important. Your choices will be more limited if you're confined to school term-time, and older children may be reaching the age when they're less enthusiastic about being dragged away from their friends.

As with all contact arrangements, how you and your ex divide and spend the holidays should ideally be discussed together. Both of you are probably going to want to spend as much time as possible with the children, and you may both want to take them away somewhere special – money allowing.

First, think about what you would like to do. How much time is available? And how can that time be spent? Bear in mind that young children may be upset if separated from the residential parent for long periods of time, so shorter, frequent breaks are likely to work better than long holidays. Once you've decided how you'd like the holiday period to pan out, discuss it with your ex. Then ask the children how the plans sound to them. The more planning you can do, the better. If possible, let the children know how they'll be spending their holidays for the coming year as soon as possible to avoid any anxieties or confusions.

For all of you, this first year's holidays are likely to be the hardest. Try to avoid revisiting old places where the other parent's absence may feel more noticeable, and instead go somewhere or do something completely new. You could consider an activity holiday or a beach resort if you haven't been before, or hiring a caravan. Think also about what you'll do while the children are away with the other parent so you can reassure them that you'll be fine alone. That might simply be catching up with work and household chores, or going off to visit friends.

SPECIAL OCCASIONS

Christmas, Diwali, Easter, birthdays, graduation, bar mitzvahs, etc. are all events that have to be renegotiated in the post-separated family. Again, planning ahead is not only best for the children; it also gives the parents time to make the necessary arrangements, whether they're to be with the kids or alone.

Firstly you need to think about what the children will want. Ideally, of course, they'd like both their parents to be together, and for things that are totally focused around them, such as birthdays, graduation, religious ceremonies, hopefully this is something you can agree to do. With the attention being on the child, rather than the two of you, many parents do manage to get through these events – though it may be more painful for some than others. Children will expect to spend Fathers' Day with Dad and Mothers' Day with Mum, and respective birthdays with the parent. And family occasions will depend on whose side of the family they are. But other events, such as Christmas, can be difficult. Taking alternate years often doesn't work, particularly for younger children, who will see twelve months as far too long to wait to spend Christmas with the other parent. Many couples manage to split the day and create new traditions to make their time with the children special.

For example, one mum told me that when she has the children on Christmas Eve they spend the day making sweets, share a special meal in the evening and open presents before bedtime. Their dad then has them Christmas morning through to Boxing Day with the usual present-opening and turkey dinner. And then they swap the following year. Children often enjoy creating a new ritual for Christmas, and while they still experience the loss of not having both parents together on Christmas Day, they do get two special days instead of one.

It's also worth considering seeing the children individually. Some children will want to be with their siblings while others may relish the idea of getting a parent's undivided attention. As with holidays, try to remain flexible. This is new for all of you, and it may be that next year you'll all come up with an even better way of doing things.

PRESENTS

Anyone who says you can't buy love hasn't had children! Of course the saying is true, but, as all parents know, children of any age respond positively to presents. Having said that, it's important that children don't think that presents equal love. For many families, separation brings inevitable financial constraints, and honest conversations about not being able to afford the same Christmas or birthday presents makes it clear that the issue is cash, not how much you love them.

When money's tighter and you desperately want to make your children happy, present-buying can become a very contentious issue. It's hard to hear a child's enthusiastic adoration of a parent who's just bought them something you can't afford. And if you're the parent that's just splashed out, it's painful to hear them ask if it's okay to take it

'Daddy buys us lovely presents every time we see him but we can't take them home to show Mummy or to put with our other toys. He does it because he doesn't want us to be happy in Mummy's house.'
Sam and Ellie, aged seven and five

'home'. While it's good for children to have some special items in each house, it's also essential that they feel able to take things between homes. This reinforces that both places belong to them equally and that they should feel 'at home' in both locations.

During the first year or so, it's best if parents can agree a budget for presents to save bitterness on both sides. Remember that children who are old enough to know the price of things will also feel very awkward if they've received a gift from one parent that they know will upset the other. So you're not just hurting your ex with extravagant gifts, but your child as well. It also makes sense to discuss lists with each other so you don't duplicate presents and, when possible, agree in advance what you're going to buy so there are no surprises for the parents on the big day.

SCHOOL

As discussed in Chapter 5, it's important that the children's school are aware of the fact that you and your partner have separated. Hopefully you will have told them when you first broke the news to the children, but you should also tell them when you've actually begun to live separately, so that they can be aware of any additional stress that the children may be experiencing and give the right support.

Some children may struggle to focus on school, particularly in the first year as they settle into new domestic routines, and may be more distracted or disruptive than usual. Other children throw themselves into school as a welcome haven from the hassles of home, and enjoy the firm structure and routines that school life provides.

'Everything's changed since Mum and Dad separated. All the kids in school treat me differently as I have to have free school dinners. Mum can't afford to buy me the clothes I used to have. I don't like being different.'
Jake, aged thirteen

On a practical level, you and your ex will need to ensure that both of you are kept informed of your children's progress and receive information on parents' events, sports days, open days, review evenings, etc., as well as getting the annual school report. You'll also need to discuss who will attend events. Will you attend together or at different times? Will you sit together or apart? If it's an event where your children will also be present, such as a sports day or school production, then it's considered best for children if you go separately, as seeing the two of you side by side may unwittingly fuel their dreams of reconciliation.

RECONCILIATION FANTASIES

Children of all ages are likely, either consciously or unconsciously, to continue to hold on to some hope that you will get back together. Younger children may break your heart when they blow out their birthday candles and loudly proclaim that they wished Mummy and Daddy would love each other again. Older children are less likely to verbalise these hopes, but they may remember their past 'perfect' family through rose-tinted spectacles. These fantasies are a perfectly natural coping mechanism, and it's important that you accept their feelings without giving false hope.

Dreams of reconciliation will begin to fade during the first year, particularly if you continue to answer any questions that arise about why you split up (see Chapter 5). You can help this further by making sure you're not over-familiar with your ex. By all means be civil and polite, but letting your children overhear you laughing together or having a hug can be very confusing. Some couples are tempted to continue going to events together or even on holiday for 'the sake of the children', but in reality, rather than helping them, it's more likely to delay the time it takes them to come to terms with the permanence of the separation.

Occasionally couples begin to have second thoughts themselves. The reality of the split may have left one or both of you wondering if you should give the relationship another chance. If this is the case, then under no circumstances let your children know until the two of you have made a firm decision that you're going to work at it again. And even then, be sure that you've done everything you can to maximise your chances of success. Watching your parents split up once is bad enough, so don't risk putting them through it again unless you've really thought about it.

IN-LAWS AND MUTUAL FRIENDS

One of the most difficult areas for all separated couples to manage is seeing in-laws and mutual friends. From the children's perspective it's important that they continue to have access to the support and care of all the adults in their lives, regardless of whose friend or relative they are. As well as their parents and teachers, that often includes grandparents, aunts and uncles, and close family friends. Understandably, this can sometimes cause tensions for the adults, but it can be minimised with open communication between all parties.

Try to agree with your ex what will be said to each respective parent, sibling or close friend. Agree when they will see the children and how they'll maintain other contact such as phone calls, cards and/or presents. Make sure all the adults know that you're continuing to work together as parents and that you don't want any negative thoughts or feelings being communicated to the children. If they want to express their feelings to you in private, that's fine, but confirm that nothing damaging will be discussed or mentioned in front of the kids. Explain that you don't want anything to get in the way of the children continuing a positive relationship with both of you, and therefore open conversations about the other parent should be welcomed. Under no circumstances should the children ever be made to feel awkward.

Of course, this can also raise difficult feelings for you. If you've enjoyed a close relationship with your partner's family or friends in the past, you may have to have some difficult conversations about if and how that relationship can continue. Some people will take sides, leaving either you or your partner out in the cold. If this happens, then there may be little you can do to resolve the situation. In which case, all you can do is agree with them that their negative feelings will not be shared with the children.

DATING

During the first year, hopefully you'll find yourself going out with friends, at least occasionally, and maybe you'll also find yourself back on the dating scene. This can be daunting, especially if your last relationship was a long one. But it's not half as daunting for you as it is for your children. A new love interest will often be perceived as a threat. Not only a threat to the relationship they have with you, but also a threat to their dream of reconciliation. There's more on new partners in Chapter 10 but for now, we'll just focus on dating. Basically, children will see any new person as potential competition for your love and affection, or as someone who is trying to replace their other, much-loved parent. In the early stages, it's best to keep dating low-key and away from the children. If someone is beginning to be more significant in your life, then you'll need to think about how to introduce them to your children, but until that time, it's best for everyone if your personal life remains that way – personal.

MANAGING YOUR FEELINGS

Whether you chose to end the relationship or it was forced upon you, the first year is the toughest. Not only are you struggling with the many mixed emotions after a separation, but you're also adjusting to living alone. The first year will bring many 'firsts' as a single parent – the first birthday, the first Christmas, the first holiday, the first school play. There'll also be other firsts you may not have anticipated. The first time the boiler broke down or a red sock slipped into the whites wash. The first time a distant friend rang who hadn't yet heard the news. All of these firsts are milestones

'Mum says I have to forget Dad. I just can't stop thinking about him – he's in my mind all the time.'
Daniel, aged nine

in your journey. Each is an opportunity for you to discover your strengths and resources, both as an individual and as a parent.

During this year, you should find that the rollercoaster ride of emotions begins to level out a bit. But do continue to get support for yourself, and perhaps use some of the suggestions in Chapter 2. Possibly one of the hardest things about being a single parent is having to make decisions on your own. Hopefully you and your ex can still discuss some of the major aspects of parenting, but the day-to-day decisions of running the home and how to discipline the children will now fall to you alone. It can feel very lonely, and many people find that the weight of responsibility fuels feelings of anger towards the ex. Although these feelings are totally natural, it's important that you don't let your children see you blaming an ex for the difficulties you're now facing. Doing this can leave children feeling they should also be angry at the other parent on your behalf, and can consequently damage the relationship. Remember once again that no matter how bad a partner your ex may have proved to be, they can still be an excellent parent. And during this formative first year, your children need your encouragement and support to continue a healthy relationship with their mum *and* dad.

Hearing about the ongoing relationship between your child and your ex can be painful. It's common for children to put the non-resident parent on a pedestal, and young children, who may be less aware of your feelings, may chat endlessly about what a great time they've had. Remember that whatever your feelings may be towards your ex, it's great that your child is still able to enjoy being with them. Find a friend that you can shout and cry with, and make sure your child knows that seeing them happy makes you happy.

Few parents ever seem to believe that they're doing a good job. But single parents, especially soon after separation, can struggle more than most. Some will feel an overwhelming sense of guilt that their marriage 'failed' and therefore they've let down their children. Some will throw themselves into work to try to provide more and more in an effort to replace 'normal' family life, while others will sacrifice any time for themselves in order to be 'supermum' or 'superdad'. None of this is actually going to help your children at all. What *will* help is reminding yourself that life is not perfect and the end of your relationship had nothing to do with the children. Remember also that your children are looking to you for guidance on how to manage this transitional time and the best message you can give them is: 'It's nobody's fault, we're all going to take time to adjust to the changes, and we'll all be okay.' No child really wants a 'superparent' – they want someone who's real and who loves them. Whatever age we are, we all struggle at times and we all make mistakes. If you get it wrong sometimes, then be a good role model to your children, apologise for your mistake, make amends and move on.

Dos and Don'ts
Below is a list of dos and don'ts to help you make this difficult first year easier for your children:

DO
➤ Be flexible.
➤ Let children know you'll miss them when they're with the other parent but you're going to be fine.
➤ Listen to the kids' views.
➤ Plan holidays well in advance.
➤ Maintain contact with your ex via phone or email to confirm contact arrangements, and keep these exchanges separate from time with the children.
➤ Start up new traditions and rituals for special occasions.
➤ Let children talk about visits and share their enthusiasm, but respect them if they prefer to say nothing.

➤ Decide ahead of time how you'll manage school events.
➤ Be discreet about dating.
➤ Be civil with your ex but not over-familiar, which can be confusing.
➤ Remember that this first year is difficult for everyone.

DON'T
➤ Ask children for information about the other parent.
➤ Cancel arrangements, as this leaves children thinking they're not important.
➤ Be late to collect or drop off children, as this creates increasing anxiety.
➤ Hang on to old holiday routines or special occasion traditions, as it can make the absence of the other parent more obvious.
➤ Stop your child taking things between houses.
➤ Buy presents that you know will upset your ex and therefore put your child in a difficult position.
➤ Introduce new people into your children's lives unless they're likely to be around for some time.
➤ Put down your partner in front of your children or show open hostility.
➤ Use kids as messengers.
➤ Give yourself a hard time if you make mistakes – no one is perfect!

PART III

Parenting Together when Living Apart

This section is about the complexities of continuing your parenting relationship when your couple relationship has ended. The first chapter, Chapter 9, explores problems between the parents such as communication issues as well as common difficulties that the children may have. Chapter 10 addresses children's reactions to a new partner, and offers advice on making the transition as smooth as possible. Chapter 11 is dedicated to the more complicated scenarios that some people face: the unco-operative ex, and situations that involve domestic abuse, addiction and mental health difficulties. There's an overview of legal and financial matters relating to separation and divorce in Chapter 12, including financial settlements, contact orders and the divorce process itself, as well as a section on mediation.

CHAPTER 9

Overcoming Parenting Problems

Being a parent is a tough job. It's hard work, highly responsible, untrained, unpaid, extremely demanding and regularly unappreciated. But in spite of all that, it can still be one of the most fulfilling and rewarding things you'll ever do in your life. Parenting after separation can become easier on some levels, but even harder on others.

From a practical viewpoint, separation means you each become single parents with more or less residential responsibility. You will each be responsible for the rules of your home and the way you spend time with your children. If there's a problem, then each of you will be individually responsible for how you handle it, and you alone will decide how to reward and discipline your child. For couples who've always had different views on parenting, being a single parent may be a relief. However, there are still many areas where a consistent approach from both parents will be beneficial for your child, and if you've never agreed in the past, it may be even harder to do so now.

The qualities required for effective co-parenting are good communication, compromise and co-operation. Unfortunately for many couples, these core elements may never have existed within the relationship. If you've always struggled to talk as a couple then the emotional stress of separation may make communication even harder. And even if you have been fairly good at talking about things in the past, if one of you is still really upset or angry about the separation, it could take some time for those old skills to return.

Some couples are surprised to discover that they communicate better when apart than they did when they lived together. Once the separation is complete and the focus of conversations is purely on the children, many couples realise that for everyone concerned, you might as well get on with the job of being parents and leave bad feelings in the past.

> **'As soon as we finally split up, the arguing stopped. I think we both realised there was no point any more, so we just got on with it.'**
> **Heather, mother of two**

HOW TO COMMUNICATE WITH YOUR EX

Calmness and courtesy are perhaps the two most important words to remember when communicating with your ex. Whatever the subject may be, think about how you would speak to someone at work or in a shop if you needed to share or obtain information, or if you had a problem you wanted to resolve. You certainly wouldn't be angry and abusive, rake up the past or start talking about irrelevant issues. And if a stranger came to speak to you, you wouldn't tut, roll your eyes or get irritated; you would listen and try to help if at all possible.

Another essential ingredient of good communication is to give your ex the benefit of the doubt and always assume the best. Even if past experience tells you that they're likely to be negative or obstructive, remember that circumstances are different now and people do change. If you're expecting a no, the worst that can happen is that you'll be right, but for the sake of moving forward as co-operating parents, it's well worth the risk that they might say yes.

When couples are able to communicate well about parenting issues it shows children that they are willing to put their differences to one side in order to look after them. It says that the children are the priority.

As discussed before, most potentially difficult situations can be avoided by planning ahead and agreeing rules and roles beforehand. Chapter 8 looked at agreeing contact arrangements and handover times, holidays and present-giving. You may also want to agree basic rules for behaviour – for example, bedtimes, coming-in times, chores and homework routines. Some children find it easier to have the same rules in each house, though most will easily adapt if they are different. Children are used to there being different rules at school, after-school clubs, or in Grandma's house, and can usually accommodate different rules at Mum's and Dad's.

A lot of communication can also be done in a non-direct environment. For example, emailing, online chat, telephone or texting. Talking in these kinds of environments can often feel less confront-ational and consequently can be more emotion-free. However, be aware that things that have been written can easily be misread, so make sure you're clear about what you're trying to say.

'I still find it difficult to talk to her without getting angry so we do everything via Friday emails.' Dave, father of three, fourteen months after separation

If you do need to speak in a face-to-face environment then make sure it's a convenient time for both of you, and that you have sufficient time and energy to address the issue in hand. Be clear in your mind about what you want to say and the outcome you'd like to reach. Remember to be ready to compromise and give your ex the benefit of the doubt. You may also find the following guidelines useful:

LISTEN ATTENTIVELY

The first rule of good communication is listening. When you're listening, don't just listen with your ears. Show your ex that you're really listening by giving them 100 per cent of your attention.

CHECK OUT

Make sure that you're hearing what your ex is saying by checking out important details. If necessary, interrupt them and say, 'So you're saying that…' When you hear them reply 'exactly' – you'll both know you've heard right.

EMPATHISE

Show that you're willing to see things from their perspective by putting yourself in their shoes. Saying 'I can understand that this is difficult/frustrating/upsetting for you…' conveys that you're not just thinking about yourself.

EXPLAIN YOURSELF

When you're talking, be ready to give as much information as your ex needs to understand your point of view. Remember that if you're talking about what your children want you'll need to back it up with facts; otherwise, it's just your opinion.

EXPRESS YOURSELF

As well as giving the facts, say how you and the children are feeling. But make sure the feelings are directly relevant to the point you're trying to make and support that point.

KEEP EMOTIONS IN CHECK

If you're aware of emotions rising as you speak, try to keep them in check. It's understandable that you may feel old feelings of anger or upset resurfacing, but remember that the goal of your conversation is to resolve something for your children's benefit, not to share your feelings about the relationship or the separation.

BE ADULT

Make sure you don't slip into behaving like a child, by sulking, whining, blaming or being obstinate. And don't fall into the trap of becoming a critical parent, by condescending, criticising or punishing. Speak like an adult – calm, focused, listening and negotiating.

If things do start to get out of hand and tensions begin to rise, then the best thing is to agree to a 'time out'. If one or both of you is getting angry then it's unlikely that you'll be able to resolve the problem constructively. Agree to come back to the discussion on another occasion when both of you have had time to calm down and think about what's been said. And, more importantly, when both of you have had time to think about what will be in the best interests of your children.

> *Violence or threats of violence are never okay. If conversations are always aggressive, or if you're avoiding resolving issues because you're scared of things getting out of control, then you should seek help at once. There's more advice on this in Chapter 11.*

If your ex is always angry when you speak to them then the most important thing to remember is that when someone has lost their temper, they are not being rational. There is no point trying to use reason. Your goal can only be to keep your cool and calm the situation – not to resolve the issue. The following tips may help you to manage their anger more effectively and constructively:

KEEP CALM

Anger fuels anger, so staying composed yourself can help to calm a situation. You could also choose to talk in a peaceful environment where it's harder to lose your temper such as a quiet café or restaurant, or a public park.

ACKNOWLEDGE YOUR EX'S FEELINGS

Openly saying 'I can see you're angry' and, if appropriate, 'I understand you're angry about...' will prevent your ex from feeling that they have to prove how they feel.

SHOW YOU'RE LISTENING

People often continue to be angry because they don't think they're being listened to or taken seriously. Prevent this by giving eye contact, nodding, repeating significant words and summarising what's been said.

BROKEN RECORD

This technique can help you to focus on the children's needs and to keep calm. Often an angry person will jump from one point or criticism to another without taking time to listen to what you're saying. Simply repeat, calmly, but assertively, the point you are trying to make. You can do this at the same time as using other tips. For example, 'I can see you're angry, but we still have to change this for the children's sake' or 'I'm sorry that you're angry about changing things, but we still have to do it for the children's sake.'

SHARE YOUR FEELINGS AND FEARS

If you're feeling angry, too, then say so. If you're feeling nervous or upset by their anger, then share that also. Let your ex know that you also struggle with emotions but in spite of that you're still able to talk calmly in order to resolve things for your children.

FOGGING

This technique can be very helpful to fend off unreasonable criticism. Rather than arguing with your ex, and possibly escalating the anger, you choose to agree to some extent. For example, 'You're always changing arrangements without thinking of me' could be met with 'Perhaps I don't always think enough ahead of time.' Or 'You're always spoiling the children to make me feel small' could be answered by saying, 'Sometimes I do spend too much and I know that affects you.'

NEGATIVE ASSERTION

When the criticism is genuine, it can be natural to argue back or try to justify ourselves. Negative assertion simply means calmly and seriously agreeing with what's been said. This technique can stop an angry outburst in its tracks. For example, 'You're so inconsiderate, you're late again' and 'Yes, that was inconsiderate of me.'

BE CONCILIATORY

Say something that will show your ex you want to make peace. For example, you could apologise (if appropriate), acknowledge your part in the problem, show regret that the separation has happened (even if it was out of your control), or offer a compromise.

POSITIVE SELF-TALK

Last, and by no means least, if your ex is regularly angry, you need to look after your own self-esteem. You may have lived with an angry person for many years, and that sort of environment can wear anyone down. Remind yourself that you are an okay person and your ex's anger is their problem now, not yours.

Whatever your communication dilemmas may be, don't be tempted to use your child as a go-between. Making your children relay messages may save you angst but it creates untold burdens for them. Even if the information is neutral and non-contentious, it forces the children to be part of your adult, parenting relationship. And if the information is sensitive, they are forced to experience the pain of witnessing the reaction of the other parent.

If conflict is becoming regular, but there is still something important that you need to resolve, then you may find that family counselling or mediation will help. There's more information on these services in Chapter 12.

COMMON PARENTING PROBLEMS

There are several issues that may arise in the post-separation family, many of which will be part of the everyday experience of growing up. Let's face it, all kids can be difficult at times, even downright impossible. But when there are two parenting households, kids have extra worries and also extra ammunition to throw at you.

Firstly it's essential to identify exactly what the issue is. For example, if little Billy angrily screams, 'I hate you, I want to live with my dad!' when you've finally got him off the PlayStation and dragged him upstairs to brush his teeth ready for bed, it could be one of a number of issues: 1) I was really enjoying that game and didn't want to stop; 2) I hate the fact that I have to do what you say; 3) I hate you for spoiling my game and want to punish you by saying something hurtful; 4) Dad always lets me stay up late so I wish I was with him right now; 5) I'd prefer to live with Dad; or something else such as 6) I'm nervous about school tomorrow and don't want to go to bed.

In reality it may be a combination of all of the above, but what's important is that you take time to explore what the real issue is and not automatically assume it's number five.

Post-separation is an anxious time for most parents, and it's easy to assume that every behavioural change and parenting dilemma is a result of the relationship breakdown. But this is often not the case. In many cases the issue is one that every parent struggles with, and while your situation may be a contributory factor, or make resolving the issue more complicated, it is not the cause.

Below is a list of common protests that children from separated families often make, along with some advice from Angela Holland at Parentline Plus, the national charity that supports parents and carers:

> *'I was convinced my thirteen-year-old daughter was struggling to come to terms with the divorce because her behaviour became so bad. Talking to friends and to her helped me to realise that 99 per cent of it was just normal teenage rebellion.'*
> *Cathy, mother of one*

'I WANT TO LIVE WITH DAD/MUM'

As shown above, this protest is one that's commonly thrown at the resident parent in the heat of an argument or angry outburst, and is often not really meant. However, if your child says this regularly, or as part of a non-heated conversation, then you need to address it. Wanting to live with the other parent is of course very natural. As we've explored earlier in this book, the majority of children wish they could live with both parents together, so it's really not surprising that sometimes they'll miss the other parent and want to live with them. But bear in mind that 'I want to live with my dad/mum' doesn't necessarily equal 'I don't want to live with you.'

Sometimes, living with the other parent just isn't a possibility, and your child will need to understand this. Reassure them that you both love them equally but it's not practical for them to live with the other parent. If your ex can also reinforce this message, then that will help. However, if your ex is offering this as a realistic option, then the situation is trickier. In many cases, taking time to explore what your child is really wanting and finding other ways to fulfil some of those needs, such as increased contact time with the other parent, will help. And if you're going through a particularly difficult patch in your relationship with your child, it is a good idea to explain that going to the other parents won't resolve it. Instead, encourage them to work with you to make the situation at home better.

If your ex can realistically offer your child residence, and you believe your child is old enough and mature enough to make that decision, then you may need seriously to consider letting them go. Obviously this decision should not be taken lightly, and the three of you should take all the necessary time to consider the pros and cons, and also what you'll do if things don't work out.

Angela says: 'It is very easy to get caught up in feelings of hurt, resentment and anger, and moving from ex-partners to co-parents can be a difficult transition to make. Parents want the best for their children, which doesn't always translate into what is best for the parent. There are lots of variables that will influence decisions, including the age of the children, the distance between the separated couple, the practicalities of the accommodation itself, educational needs and working hours. There are leaflets and websites that can help. Separating the practical from the emotional can feel overwhelming, and parents may feel they need extra support. The wider family, friends, and organisations such as Parentline Plus and Relate play a vital role in this lifelong process as children grow and parents' circumstances change.'

'I DON'T WANT TO SEE MUM/DAD'

This is the opposite problem to the previous one, and there may be a number of reasons why it is being said. The most common reason is that your child has fallen out with the other parent. They may have a good reason, or it may simply be that your ex made a reasonable request or refused to let them do something and they're annoyed about it. If this is the case then you need to tell them that the only way to overcome these sorts of problems is to face them head on, not to run away from them.

Another common reason not to want to see the other parent is because they find the experience upsetting in some way. Either upsetting when they're there or upsetting when they get home. In this case you need to find out exactly what's going on and see if it can be resolved. It may be that it's something that you're doing, or something your ex is doing. If it's the latter, then, depending on the age of the child, you could encourage them to speak to your ex about it, or you could approach him or her on their behalf.

If this protest is coming from teenagers it could simply be apathy. The nature of adolescence is that parents become less and less important as their social life becomes increasingly active. Try not to take their rejection personally, and encourage them to consider the impact of their decision on the other parent.

Angela says: 'It is really important that, although children know their parents are separated and no longer want to live together, they are entitled to have a relationship with both. Children need their parents to understand that they can love both of them without feeling disloyal to the other one. Relationships may need building, so it is worth thinking about the different ways in which contact can take place between visits so that the relationship feels everyday rather than short bursts of intense time spent together. Phone, email, texts and letters can help with this. If you have left the family home, you may need to show your child that although you don't live with them any more you still love them very much. Offer lots of reassurance, and be patient with them as they come to terms with the changes. Contact arrangements need to be reviewed regularly as your child grows and their needs change, and they will have their own views on this.'

'DAD/MUM LETS ME'

In nearly all separated families there will be different rules in different houses, and this can be frustrating for children. However, as we said earlier, most children can adjust to this over time, and would generally prefer for one house to be more lenient than run the risk of them both becoming strict! Rules also tend to be different when the circumstances are different. For example, the parent who just has the children at the weekend is bound to be more lenient about bedtimes, and unlikely to ask them to contribute to household chores. The weekend parent also often gets to do the fun leisure stuff while the weekday parent has to consider school routines and homework as well. This is not only 'unfair' on the children, but also on the parents. Sharing this disparity with children can help them to understand why things are different and to be more accepting of the other's household rules.

'My daughter knows that the best way to hurt me is to say she wants to live with dad. I know she doesn't really mean it, but it cuts every time she says it.'
Puja, mother of four

It can be tempting to get caught into a competition and, in your efforts to defend your own rules, inadvertently put down the other parent. Think about why you have the rules that you have and stick to these. The broken record technique may help you to not get caught up in a battle with the other parent. For example, 'I know Daddy lets you stay up later, but when you're here you have to go to bed at 7.00pm,' and continuing, 'Yes, I know it seems unfair to you because it's different at Dad's, but when you're here you have to go to bed at 7.00pm.'

If there is a massive discrepancy in a rule that you think is important, then you might decide you want to broach this with your ex. If you do so, make sure it's not in front of your child, and at a time that's convenient for both of you. Remember that you can only put your point of view across. For example, children should brush their teeth *every* night, but at the end of the day, the rules you set in your own home will be entirely up to you.

Angela says: 'Playing one parent off against the other is a common experience not only for separated parents but parents who are still together, so communication is key when setting some basic ground rules. It can feel understandably frustrating if the kids are tired and irritable because they have been allowed to stay up late, or you are struggling to get their homework done late on a Sunday night because it hasn't been done at the weekend. It can be equally frustrating if you want to make the most of the limited time you have and want it to be quality time without the pressures of someone else's demands or rules. Some of these things can be ironed out while others will need to be tolerated, but it is important that discussions are respectful and show an understanding of the other parent's point of view.'

'JUST BECAUSE MY BROTHER/SISTER GOES, WHY DO I HAVE TO?'

Many parents worry when siblings want to do different things. Before the separation, chances are you did lots of things as a family unit, but now you're separated, there will be more fragmentation. You may feel very strongly that your children should be kept together and do things together. Part of this may be about your need to maintain some sense of family unity, rather than actually something that the children want or feel is important. Many children like to spend time alone with each parent, and a separated family allows more opportunities for that. They may dislike the feeling that they're being herded together and have to do everything at the same time. A chance to go to Dad's or Mum's alone may be beneficial for everyone.

Sometimes there are practical reasons why they need to do things at the same time, in which case you'll need to explain this. Rather than telling them that they 'should' go together, explain the reasons why you or your ex need time alone or have to see them together. If they've fallen out with their sibling, encourage them to resolve the problem and be friends again. And if they would like more independent time with each parent, see if you can negotiate a convenient time for everyone when this can happen.

> *'His mum always said I was too lenient but I reckon I've got the right to spoil him now I only see him once a fortnight.'*
> Leroy, father of two

Angela says: 'You may find that your ex's time with the kids is a great opportunity to recharge your batteries. Don't feel guilty that you want and even need this; it is important that you make time for yourself. Siblings spending one-on-one time with each parent is certainly an option that could work well for everyone.'

'I HATE MUM'S/DAD'S NEW PARTNER'

This is an extremely common problem, which is addressed in much more detail in the next chapter. When a new partner arrives on the scene, many children will feel that their divided loyalties have been split yet again. Complaints about the new partner may be much more to do with confirming their loyalty to you then expressing genuine dislike.

A new partner often dilutes the time a parent spends with their children, and this is probably the biggest issue that children have. Or it may be that they resent seeing this virtual stranger being comfortable in their home. Taking time to help your child understand what the issue is about will help them to rationalise it in their own mind. It may also help them to think about if and how they could talk to their other parent about the issue.

Many parents struggle when they discover that their ex is seeing someone new, and hearing about them from your child can be very painful. Difficult as it may be, try to be as neutral as you can about the situation in front of your child, and encourage them to discuss any issues with the other parent. And while they're doing that, get some support for yourself if necessary.

Angela says: 'If your ex has met someone new it is important to acknowledge your feelings and talk to a friend or a support organisation like Parentline so that your child doesn't feel caught in the middle. Restrain yourself from asking your child lots of questions about the new partner. If the relationship becomes serious and the new partner is spending lots of time with your children, you may want to meet him or her, but it is important to remember they are not part of your history or any pain you have felt, and it is far better for your children if you can be civil and work together for their sake. If you have formed a new stepfamily there are lots of ways in which you can make it work – from introducing a new partner, to how they fit into the newly formed family. Children need lots of reassurance and time to adjust. Parent and step-parents need to support each other and keep the lines of communication open.'

There are probably countless other issues that will crop up over the coming months and years as your children grow and their family life continues to change. No one is a perfect parent, and all you can hope for is to do your best for them. Remember that whatever the reasons for the separation, this is a difficult time for everyone, but you can continue to be a loving, thriving family.

CHAPTER 10

New Partners

Sooner or later, either you or your partner is likely to meet someone else. The timing of this new union is extremely important. Ideally, you shouldn't consider introducing anyone new into your life until both you and your children have adjusted to the separation and the new lifestyle of having separate parents in separate homes. Your children need time to accept that your relationship with the other parent is over and there's no chance of reconciliation. If a partner is introduced too early, children are more likely to feel they are a replacement for the other parent.

Suzie Hayman, author of *The Relate Guide to Second Families* and counsellor on the BBC's *Stepfamilies* series, says: 'Of course, real life doesn't always go to plan, and you may find yourself falling head over heels in love and wanting to combine lives with a new person as soon as possible. However reasonable or desirable this feels, thinking of your children's reactions and needs may help you take it at a slower and more measured, planned pace.'

However, the ending of your relationship may have been triggered by meeting someone else. In the majority of situations when this happens there were already problems in the relationship, and someone new is the catalyst for bringing the relationship to an end. But from your children's perspective, and possibly from your ex's as well, this new person may be seen as the cause of the break-up. In order for your new partner to be accepted as part of your future family structure, you should try to ensure that you have time living separately while your children adjust. This will help them to see the relationship break-up and your new partner as distinct and separate events.

UNDERSTANDING CHILDREN'S REACTIONS

Most children want their parents to be happy. And most realise that, in part, means meeting someone new. However, while they may want you and your ex to meet someone else, they may also struggle with the impact that will have on their relationship with you. If you've been single for a while, they may be used to having you to themselves. Indeed, many parents become particularly close to their children after a relationship breakdown, so it's especially hard for them to see you getting close to someone else. Feelings of jealousy are natural, and your children will need your help to understand that a couple relationship is different from their relationship with you, and that you will not love them any less because of it.

> *'I always wanted Mum to meet someone new. I just wish she'd waited till I'd left home.'* Charlotte, aged fourteen

A new partner also signals the end of any reconciliation fantasies that your children may have had. As discussed in previous chapters, it's common for children to cling to the hope that one day Mum and Dad will get back together. The introduction of a new partner means the end of those dreams, and may rekindle feelings of loss.

Some children can feel afraid that a new partner will get in the way of their relationship with the other parent. They may become angry and resentful, and spend a lot of time making comparisons between the two. If they particularly like the new partner, they may struggle with feelings of disloyalty and go to great lengths to act as if they don't like them, which can be very confusing for everyone.

When just one parent has a new partner, children can become anxious for the other, single parent. They may become more acutely aware that the other parent is alone, and want to spend more time with them to prevent them from feeling lonely.

Suzie Hayman adds: 'Children living with separation or divorce often take on the role of carers, or parents, to their parents. They worry about them, care for them and even feel responsible for them. They may see themselves as the missing parent's representative and that it's their job to act as, or in the interests of, the other parent. They can see an incoming adult as a rival, challenging their position, and so feel it's their place to resist invasion or takeover.'

All of these feelings are very natural and will pass in time if they are handled sensitively. Children just need to feel they can share their fears and anxieties, and that they are supported in adjusting to change.

THE FIRST INTRODUCTION

We looked briefly at dating in Chapter 8 and talked about the importance of keeping casual liaisons as low-key as possible within family time. But once you've met someone you want to be a part of your everyday life, then it's time to consider how to introduce them to your children.

Start by casually mentioning in conversation that you've met someone. Make them aware when you're going out to meet them, and let their natural curiosity begin to build. Over a relatively short period of time, depending on the age of your children, they'll probably begin to ask questions: What's he/she like? Where do they live? Do they have children? How old are they? Are you going to get married? Yes – your children are likely to get to the nitty-gritty much earlier than you think. The deeper question underpinning all these is: How much impact is this person going to have on my life?

Be as honest as you can in answering their questions, and reassure them that you're not going to make any changes in their life without giving them plenty of warning. Also encourage them to recognise that relationships take time to build and no one's sure how they'll turn out in the long run. Once they've begun to ask questions, ask if they'd like to meet them. If they say no, be aware that this may be out of loyalty to your ex. Within reason, give them as much time as they require. But if you feel they could procrastinate for ever, then you may need gently to push things forward.

Whenever the introduction happens, make sure it's low-key. A first meeting will often work best around an activity where there's an additional focus other than the meeting itself. For example, tenpin bowling or a trip to the park. Subsequent meetings should build gradually on this and be taken at your children's pace. You do need to spend time with a new partner in normal, everyday contact, as well as fun trips and treats. Otherwise, children start expecting that it will always be fun and games, and find it a shock when reality bites.

If you're the resident parent and you're still living in the family home, then you must be aware of how it will feel for the children when your new partner visits the house. If possible, let the children get to know your new partner away from home at first, and when they first visit, make it brief. As the length of their visits to your home increases, try to avoid slipping into any familiar routines, such as your new partner sitting in your ex's chair or always being the one to decide what to watch on TV. This will help to re-emphasise the fact that your new partner is in no way replacing the other parent.

If you're a non-resident parent, then make sure your new partner isn't always with you during contact times. Remember that your children will want to maximise the limited time they have with you, and may quickly resent it if they feel that time is being diluted by someone else.

The most important thing to remember when introducing a new partner is to take things slowly and sensitively. Remember that this is yet another family change for children. One that they didn't choose. In the long-term, a new partner can be a benefit to everyone, but in the short-term, your children need your support and help to adjust.

> '**We went to the pub like we always did and there she was. Dad said, "This is Claire. You've all got to be nice to her."'**
> **Kate, aged nine**

Whatever you do, don't surprise your kids with your new partner. Remember that no matter how excited or enthusiastic you may be about your new relationship, they're a stranger to your kids, and possibly an unwanted one.

MOVING FORWARD TOGETHER

Some couples decide quite quickly that they would like to set up home together and form a new, step or second family. As adults, this may make a lot of sense, practically as well as emotionally, but for any children involved, it can be a daunting proposition.

There isn't room in this chapter thoroughly to explore all the ins and outs of stepfamily life, but hopefully it can give you an overview of how your children may feel, as well as some first steps in helping everyone adjust

Children are much more likely to be suspicious of a new partner if they think they're being kept in the dark. Make sure you include children in planning new arrangements, and keep them informed of what's going on and how their new family life will be.

Suzie Hayman continues: 'Including kids in plans isn't the same as giving them the right to make choices for you. It doesn't actually help children to be told: "I won't do this if it makes you unhappy." But it's worth being aware of the fact that the main factor that really hurts children in separation, divorce and re-partnering is the fact that they are spectacularly out of control of the process – it's your choice not theirs. So since you can't give them power in this area, make a point of giving them choices and control of other areas of their lives in compensation: choice of rooms, choice of decoration, choice of what the family should do together one night a week.'

If you're a resident parent and your new partner is moving into your house, then be aware that the children may feel as though their home is being invaded by a stranger. Think about how you can continue to let them have their own space, and make any adjustments to the layout and contents of the home gradually. If you're moving into a new home together, then make sure the children are fully involved so it feels like everybody's house.

If you're a non-resident parent then your children may feel quite strange about having to go to a home where someone else also lives. They will probably have got used to being at Dad's or Mum's, and feeling truly comfortable in a house where a new partner lives may take some time. If at all possible, try to maintain some of the old structure of contact times, and definitely make time to see them on your own.

'Dad can't see me any more. He says it's too hard on his new family.' James, aged nine

If your new partner has children of their own, even if they're not going to be living with you, your children are likely to worry about diluting available resources such as money, transport, mealtimes and sleeping arrangements. And they'll also worry about the emotional resources as well. Will there be enough love and time to go around? Make sure your children know that they will still be a priority in your life, no matter who else is in the picture.

All children have a deep desire to get on well with a new partner, whether that's a new live-in partner or one who is visited. Some children may be good at hiding this desire, but none the less, deep down they want a harmonious family life. Unfortunately, most children will have grown up with stories of wicked 'step-parents', so they'll need plenty of reassurance, as well as time to learn that these are myths, not an inevitable reality.

CREATING AND MAINTAINING HARMONY IN NEW FAMILIES

Just because you love your new partner, it doesn't mean your children will. And, equally, just because you love your children, it doesn't mean your partner will. You have had years with your children to develop a special bond – it didn't happen overnight. It is going to take time, patience and commitment from both of you to build a relationship between your children and your new partner, and to create a happy family environment.

It will be much easier to have a harmonious family life if you and your partner have spent some time thinking and planning ahead. Consistency is important for children of any age, so between you – and the children when appropriate – you need to agree some basic rules and roles. Whether you're a resident or non-resident parent, it is you that will hold the key position of authority and responsibility. You are the link between the children and your new partner, and the one that everyone will turn to for guidance. But as the adults in the house, it is the two of you that need to ensure the home runs as smoothly as possible. Take some time as a couple to think about the following:

➤ How will you manage the relationships with ex-partners, as well as your children's ongoing contact time?

➤ How will you manage your time? Including time together, time alone with your children and time as a family?

➤ What rules will you have about bedtimes, mealtimes, tidiness, homework, going out, TV watching, pocket money, and so on.

➤ How will you organise rooms in the house so everyone feels they have their 'own' space?

➤ How will you deal with finances?

➤ What arrangements will you make for visiting stepchildren and other extended family?

➤ What will you do about special occasions such as birthdays, Christmas, etc?

Remember to let the children be involved in the decisions that are going to affect them. Arrangements are much more likely to be adhered to if they've been mutually agreed.

MAINTAINING DISCIPLINE

Discipline is difficult to maintain in any family. But in stepfamilies, it is particularly complicated. Some children react to the insecurity that comes with changing family life by becoming difficult and disruptive. Understanding the underlying feelings and working together as a couple will help you through this difficult stage.

Remember that not all changes in behaviour will be because of the new family set-up. In fact, much of it is probably just 'normal'. Whether you're trying to tame a toddler, battling with a 'tweenager' or in the midst of adolescent warfare –

children are a challenge. It is the nature of growing up to push the boundaries and to test parents and other adults. And some children just have a more headstrong disposition than others. So if you're struggling with difficult behaviour, then you first need to work out what's causing it. Is this just normal growing up? Have you been unreasonable? Is your child upset about something else that is going on in their life, with friends or at school? Or is this a reaction to becoming part of a new family?

Discipline can only be effective in an atmosphere of mutual affection and respect. You will have had many years to build and nurture a relationship with your children where discipline is expected and, to a lesser or greater degree, accepted. Therefore, at least in the early days, the majority of discipline should be handled by you. Your new partner needs to develop a relationship where there is mutual respect and trust before your children will accept discipline. Once your children like your new partner, they will want to please them and behave well.

You may find it useful to keep in mind the following guidelines:

➤ It's essential that children know that the adults are a united front, even if one parent is responsible for most of the discipline. Make sure your children know that you support each other.

➤ Agree the rules in advance and confirm that everyone is clear about them. Whenever possible, include children in setting the rules.

➤ Always be consistent and stick to what has been agreed. Make sure everyone in the house lives by the same standards and knows that 'no' means 'no'.

➤ As children grow up, rules need to change, so stay flexible. And very occasionally, under special circumstances, it may be appropriate to bend a rule.

➤ Remember to be patient. It will take time for children to adjust to family change, and bad behaviour is to be expected.

➤ Most importantly, make sure all children know that rules are there because you love them and want what's best for them.

➤ Suzie Hayman talks from experience when she suggests: 'I've always found it useful to get round the "You can't tell me what to do, you're not my dad/mum" by emphasising there are house or family rules. "In this house we don't hit/swear/make a mess, etc." It also helps to emphasise that respect and rule-keeping are mutual – adults must keep them, too – and to accept that different households do have different rules. "Yes, that's okay in your dad/mum's house. In this house we…"

> 'I refuse to do anything that Pete says, on principle. He's not my real dad and he's got no right trying to act like he is.'
> Ben, aged sixteen

Children can manage this, if you don't make it a source of conflict.'

Suzie's other tips include:

➤ Listen rather than discipline. Bad behaviour is usually about bad feelings – fear, hurt, anger about the situation. Instead of punishment, the best tactic is often to concentrate on and praise good behaviour, and see the bad as a message you need to hear. Say, 'It sounds as if you're angry/hurt/worried. Let's talk about it.'

➤ Set up a Family Round Table – a time when everyone in your home gets together to set and agree rules, share out chores, settle disputes. At the same time, have a Family Night when you play games requested by the kids. Board games are far more popular than you may think!

➤ Establish family traditions – a mix of old and new. Be aware that kids cling to old traditions as a way of holding on to the past so make allowances for that. But use the opportunity to bring in new ideas that will bind you together as a new unit.

Although stepfamilies are complex, they often bring many benefits for everyone involved. Working with your partner to resolve the initial difficulties can create a special bond between you. Children gain a wider family with even more people who will care for them and support them as they grow up. And, perhaps most importantly, you are able to show your children that whatever may have happened in the past, you can have a second chance and really enjoy life again.

HELPING YOUR CHILDREN ADJUST IF YOUR EX HAS MET SOMEONE NEW

If your ex has met someone new, then your children may not be the only ones struggling to adapt. Even if you're the one that chose to end the relationship, finding out that your ex has found another partner can come as a painful shock. Most people have no idea how they're going to feel about the news until it actually happens. And if you find that you're thrown into confusion, anger and sadness, you're not alone. Give yourself the time you need to adjust to the news, and get the support of friends and family and professionals if you need to. Remember that it's much easier to help your children with their problems if you're also managing your own.

If you are struggling with the news, then be aware that this will probably make it much harder for your children to accept your ex's new partner. Your children love you and will hate to see you hurting. Any acknowledgement on their behalf of liking the new partner may be felt as a major disloyalty to you. In fact, your children may go to great lengths to tell you how much they dislike the new partner in an effort to cheer you up. Unfortunately, this often has the opposite effect of keeping the new partner constantly in your consciousness. If this is happening then tell your children that it would be easier for you not to hear their complaints and that it would be better for them to chat to someone else. Ideally they should speak to their other parent, or perhaps there's someone else they can talk to, such as a grandparent or family friend.

On the other hand, some children may say nothing at all about the new partner and very little about time spent at the other parent's home. If this is the case, then respect that they may want to keep their parents' lives separate and don't ask questions. Your own curiosity may make it tempting to quiz your children for information, but remember this puts them in a very awkward position.

If you feel your child is genuinely having problems with your ex's new partner and it is not being exacerbated in any way by your reaction, then you need to encourage them to talk directly to their other parent about it. Remember that in the long run, it's going to be much better for children if they do get on with the new partner and therefore, painful as it may be, you should try to help them improve the situation.

CHAPTER 11

When Your Ex Won't or Can't Co-operate

Unfortunately not all parents are able to put the needs of their children above their own. That may be because of unresolved anger or guilt, or because of their very real struggle to manage their loss and come to terms with what's happened. In some cases it may be due to a mental health issue or a substance addiction or you may be breaking away from a violent or abusive relationship. Every situation will be completely different but hopefully what follows will be helpful. Remember also to take advice from other appropriate agencies in your area.

WHEN YOUR EX REFUSES TO SEE THE CHILDREN

There are a number of reasons why a parent may decide that they don't want to see their children. The first is that they cannot cope with the change of living arrangements, and the comparatively little contact leaves them feeling angry or depressed. They may decide that rather than go through the pain of missing their children, they will stop seeing them altogether. They may reason that while the sudden cut-off will be painful, everyone will get over it and move on.

Some parents may be feeling particularly bad or personally responsible about the relationship break-up, and decide that their children will be better off without them. It could be that contact is being withheld to punish the other parent. In their anger over either the breakdown or contact arrangements, they decide that the best way to hurt you is to refuse to see the children. A variation of this is to use contact with the children as a bargaining tool: 'Unless I can see them every weekend, I won't see them at all.' Finally some parents will stop seeing their children because they want to pursue a child-free life. They may feel that their parenting responsibilities ended with the relationship and prefer to move on with their life, childless.

Of course, in all these situations the person who is really hurt is the child. It may be tempting for you to decide that your children are better off without an unreliable parent, but in actual fact, they will almost certainly prefer some contact, however limited, than none at all. Try the communication techniques from Chapter 9 with your partner, and if they don't work you could talk to a trusted friend or relative of theirs to see if they can talk some sense into them. In the meantime, try to explain to your children that the other parent does still love them but they're struggling to see them right now. Do your best to keep whatever lines of contact open that you can, and encourage your children to continue talking. Hopefully, in time, things will change. If they don't, then ultimately you may have to break the news to your children that Mum or Dad won't or can't be in contact right now.

It's an unfortunate fact that some people are just not very good at being parents, and you may have to help your child to recognise that their parent is one of them. Reassure them that he or she still loves them, and make sure they know that they've not stopped seeing them because of anything they've done or not done. Hopefully, Mum or Dad will change their mind one day, and realise what they're missing.

WHEN YOUR EX STOPS YOU FROM SEEING THE CHILDREN

If your ex is stopping you from having contact with your children and is refusing to negotiate on the matter, then you may have little choice than to go through the court system. Again, try the communication tips in Chapter 9 and also see if there's a third party who can mediate for you, but if they're stubbornly refusing then the courts may be the only choice. For some parents a court order makes little difference and an angry spouse continues to withhold contact in spite of it being in the best interests of the children to see both parents. Unfortunately, although the courts do have the power to fine or imprison someone who continually breaks the court order, they rarely take this extreme measure. You'll find more legal advice in Chapter 12.

Whatever course of action you decide to take, in the short-term try to maintain indirect contact via telephone, text message, email or letters and cards, and also through extended family members and friends if possible. Make sure your children continue to know that you love them and want to be a part of their lives. In the majority of cases, when the acrimony of the separation begins to subside, contact will be resumed. And even if this doesn't happen, if you can continue to be available for your children, they will almost certainly make the decision for themselves once they're old enough to do so.

WHEN YOUR EX SEEMS DETERMINED TO MAKE LIFE DIFFICULT

Unfortunately there are some ex-partners who seem to want to do whatever they can to make life as difficult as possible for you. They may be busy every time you want to speak, refuse to return phone calls or answer emails. They may be constantly late for everything and deride every attempt you make to do things in the best interests of the children.

It may be that they've never taken things seriously, and have always been deliberately obstructive or awkward, and perhaps that's why the relationship ended. Unfortunately it's unlikely that they're going to change their behaviour now. However, it may be that this is new behaviour for them and it's their way of demonstrating their anger or frustration at the situation. Or perhaps they're so overwhelmed by the sadness of the separation that they are genuinely incapable of functioning properly.

Occasionally an ex will be overtly destructive. They may tell the children facts about the separation that are not in their best interests – for example, the details of an affair. Or they may lie about you or the circumstances of the separation in order to gain the children's allegiance. If this is happening, then it's almost certainly being done out of anger as a way of getting at you and with little thought for the impact on the children. Some may choose to persuade themselves that the children 'deserve to know the truth', and refuse to accept that it could possibly do them any harm.

Whatever the reason for the difficulties, it's hugely frustrating for you and potentially damaging for the children. It may be that using some of the tips in Chapter 9 will help to alleviate the situation. In addition you could, as suggested above, consider talking to a close friend of your ex or someone that they respect, perhaps a parent or family friend, to see if they can talk to them about the impact their behaviour is having on the children. Or it may be that a third person will be willing to act as a go-between to pass the necessary information between you.

As with the other scenarios, it's important that you don't show too much of your frustration and anger in front of your children. Remember that it's detrimental for them to feel that they have to take sides. Even if your partner is trying to get them on his or her side, it's essential that you don't retaliate with a counter attack. As difficult as it may be, you need to maintain a stance of neutrality. Continue to tell your children that you love them and this is a difficult time for everyone. You can say that Mum and Dad don't agree on the best way to handle things and that's why you're doing things differently. But the important thing is that the children still feel equally loved and wanted by both of you. Chances are that, in time, your children will see that your ways are more constructive and helpful for everyone involved, and begin to challenge the unco-operative parent.

WHEN THERE'S AN ADDICTION PROBLEM

There are many different sorts of addictive and compulsive behaviours. Alcohol, drugs, gambling, sex or work can all take over someone's life and ruin a relationship. A time of crisis, such as separation, can often make addictive patterns worse – at least in the short-term – and may add extra stress to an already very difficult time.

If your ex-partner has accepted their addiction problem, then hopefully they're getting help from an agency who may also be able to advise them on their continuing role as a parent. Or you may, like many people, suffer the misfortune of having an ex-partner who refuses to acknowledge the problem.

Either way, you'll need to make a decision – together or separately – about how much you'll tell the children. If you make that decision on your own, then you may also need to consider whether or not to tell your ex what you've told the children. It may be that their addiction had already been obvious to the children. Remember that children often know a lot more than you think and may not be at all surprised if their thoughts are then confirmed. In fact, they may be relieved that the reality of the addiction is now out in the open where it can be talked about.

An older child may be able to handle hearing that a parent has an addiction problem, while a younger child may find it confusing and frightening. Each child may need different amounts of information, delivered in age-appropriate ways.

With regard to contact, you will first need to decide whether or not the addiction puts your child at any risk. If you think it could, then you'll find more help with this in Chapter 12. If not, then you can continue with contact in the ways discussed previously.

Perhaps one of the biggest problems with an addiction is the unreliability that often goes with it. If the addiction has been around for some time, then your children are probably already aware that their mum or dad can be fickle. Or it may be that you've managed to cover up for them in the past and the children have remained relatively unaffected. Once the children are seeing the parent independently you will no longer have the same level of control over the situation and may need to talk to the children about what they should do if an unforeseen situation arises. The reality is that you will not be able to protect your children from your partner's addiction; you can only equip them as best you can in order to minimise the impact.

You may be able to find additional support through your local alcohol or drug advisory service.

WHEN THERE ARE MENTAL HEALTH DIFFICULTIES

As a society, we still seem to struggle with mental health issues. Depression and conditions on the autism spectrum are gradually becoming more accepted, but other conditions such as bipolar, schizophrenia, personality disorders and suicidal ideation are still relatively misunderstood.

Your relationship may have broken down because of a mental health problem, or you may have split up for a whole range of other reasons. Either way, your partner's mental health is probably going to be of greater concern to you during this difficult time. If the condition has been formally diagnosed and your partner is receiving treatment, then hopefully the mental health professional will be able to give both of you additional advice and support during this time. If, however, your partner is not receiving any help, then you may feel as if you have to handle everything on your own.

It's important to remember that you're not responsible for your partner's mental health, but that you are responsible for helping your children to manage the situation and to have the best possible relationship with your ex. If your children are not aware of the mental health problems, then you will need to decide how much is appropriate to tell them and when. This is going to vary from child to child and from situation to situation. You will also need to think about appropriate contact. Without you being present, you may feel more concerned about your child's emotional or even physical well-being while with their other parent. You may decide that it's necessary for them to be more aware of your partner's condition so that they can easily ask for help if necessary. Ideally you can talk all these issues through with your partner as well and decide together what to say. But if they won't talk about it, or it causes too much stress for them, which exacerbates their condition, then you may have to make those decisions alone.

You may find it helpful to get some extra support for yourself. Many of the mental health organisations, such as MIND, provide support for partners. Talking through the issues with a specialist can give you extra confidence.

WHEN THERE'S DOMESTIC ABUSE OR VIOLENCE

If your partner has been violent or abusive, then both you and your children may be at increased risk during the time of separation, and in some cases this will be an ongoing problem. Your first priority must be to keep yourself and your children safe.

Families often keep domestic abuse hidden but it is important to tell someone what is happening, and to seek help and information so that you can get the support and legal protection that you may need to protect your family and reduce the risk from further abuse. Remember the point of separation and the period after you leave are the most dangerous times in an abusive relationship, and you should seek help as soon as possible.

For help and information about all aspects of domestic abuse and your options, you can contact Women's Aid (either online or by calling the twenty-four-hour freephone number 0808 2000 247). *The Survivor's Handbook* has detailed information including how to make a safety plan, where you can get emergency or temporary accommodation, your rights to legal protection, how to try to make safe contact arrangements for children after separation, and many more things.

With regard to contact, you will need to decide whether you feel that your children will be at risk if they continue to see their other parent, and how to arrange any contact so that it is safe. If you do feel your children or yourself are at risk after separation, you will need to seek legal advice and support to organise any contact safely through the courts and make sure that this is arranged alongside any other legal protection that you may need through court orders or police action. Remember that domestic violence is a crime, and you and your children have a right to be protected.

Getting help and support from Women's Aid can also put you in contact with other survivors of domestic abuse as well as expert help. This can help you deal with the feelings of guilt, shame, loss, and hopelessness that survivors of abuse often feel, and help you understand the patterns of coercive and controlling behaviour that you have experienced, psychological as well as physical.

In addition, you'll need to consider what to say to your children. If your children have witnessed or heard abuse and/or violence then telling them the truth is the best way forward. You may think that they're not aware, but research suggests that 90 per cent of children are either in the same or next room, often know what is going on and feel powerless to help, or sometimes that they are to blame. It is important that they know that only the perpetrator is responsible for the abuse. Deciding what to say is very difficult and will, of course, depend on the age and maturity of your children, and on your individual circumstances. But it's certainly worth bearing in mind that they may know a lot more than you think. If you have discussed the abuse with your children, and they are old enough to read, you may also want to help them access www.thehideout.co.uk, a website set up by Women's Aid specifically to help children living with domestic violence.

You can get more help for yourself from either a Relate counsellor or from local Women's Aid support services, some of whom offer counselling and self-help groups. You may find that just one or two sessions will help you during this difficult time, or you may want to work with a counsellor for longer to work through your feelings about the abuse and help you to move on.

Making it easier for the kids

➤ When talking about your ex, be sure to separate out any negative behaviour from them as a person. Remember that your child shares the same genes and therefore criticising them as a person is like criticising half of your child.

➤ If it's not safe for direct contact, consider indirect contact such as letters, email, texts and phone calls.

➤ Continue to reassure children that they're not to blame.

➤ Make sure children are aware that any addictive, mental health or abusive behaviour was around before the break-up.

➤ Continue to tell them that the other parent loves them, in spite of any behaviour to the contrary.

➤ Get extra support for yourself.

➤ Try to keep your feelings of anger and powerlessness separate from your children when you need to focus on their needs.

➤ Share your hope that one day things will improve – even if sometimes you doubt it yourself.

CHAPTER 12

Financial and Legal Issues

When a relationship breaks down there are many practical issues to be considered. Decisions need to be made about where children will live and with whom, how often children will see the non-resident parent, and how the children will be looked after and supported financially. In many instances these issues will be resolved between the couple with little or no legal intervention. When arrangements can be agreed amicably, not only does this save a huge amount of stress (and money) for all involved, but it also means that arrangements are more likely to be maintained, as well as supported by the wider family and friends. However, when powerful emotions are involved, couples sometimes find it impossible to agree.

If you can't see eye to eye, then your first option could be to consider a couple of sessions with a Relate counsellor to look specifically at the parenting issues. They will help you put emotions on one side for a while and look at the essential decisions that need to be made. Alternatively – or if that has not helped – you could consider mediation.

MEDIATION

Mediation aims to help you and your partner reach decisions that are fair for both of you and are in the best interests of the children, without having to go through the courts. In fact, many solicitors and courts will recommend that you go to a mediation service to resolve your differences rather than going through a lengthy legal procedure.

Mediation sessions usually last around an hour and will focus on the practical issues of finance, dividing of property and arrangements for the children. Most people attend between two and six sessions, and at the end a written summary is produced. Your solicitor can use this document to advise you on the appropriate legal formalities, which may need to be taken to make your agreement legally binding. Your solicitor may also, if necessary, provide you with advice in the mediation process, if you feel this will help you to be more informed.

For mediation to work, both you and your ex must be willing to attend and to share all the necessary information about your situation, such as financial details and new living arrangements. If mediation breaks down, or one of you is unwilling to attend, then arrangements will need to be agreed between you and your ex's solicitors.

If you want to use mediation, then there are a number of ways that you can find out what's available in your area and if there are any charges. Firstly you can contact your local Relate centre and see if they have a mediation service. Relate mediators are also trained in the psychological and emotional impact of divorce, so this may be particularly helpful if emotions are running high. If there isn't a Relate service in your area, then you can get a list of local mediators from the UK College of Family Mediators or from your solicitor.

Mediation can result not only in a saving of legal fees, but can ultimately help to reduce hostility, tension and misunderstandings between couples. This, in turn, helps to foster better communications and relations in the future, which is so important to many couples, especially those with children. If you've been through mediation and still can't agree an amicable way forward, then your final option is to go through the legal system.

Anna Bloor from the UK College of Mediation says: 'The most important thing to remember about mediation is that you reach your own decisions for the future of your family with the help of a skilled mediator. Mediation is voluntary and confidential. You have the freedom to discuss what is important to the two of you as parents, knowing that the content of your discussions will remain confidential unless there are serious issues relating to the safety of a child or adult. You can attend mediation whenever you need to. This can be when you first separate, at the time of divorce, after court proceedings have started, or long after you have separated or divorced – for example, if you need to renegotiate arrangements for your children when you form a new relationship. Public funding is available for mediation.'

LEGAL INTERVENTION

There are three key areas that may benefit from legal intervention. They are:

1. The residence/contact arrangements for children.

2. The financial agreement – including splitting of assets, financial support for each parent, and financial support for the children.

3. The divorce or separation agreement.

Each of these three areas is closely interlinked, but for the sake of clarity we will look at them individually in this chapter. All the information has been kindly provided by Resolution, the organisation specialising in family law. All the details were accurate at the time this book was published, but please do check before finally deciding your course of action.

CHOOSING A SOLICITOR

Whatever your situation, it's essential that you get personal, professional advice from a solicitor who is experienced in family law. A good solicitor will be able to look at your individual circumstances and advise you on the available options while ensuring that the welfare of the children comes first. Solicitors that are members of Resolution aim to help separating couples achieve a constructive settlement of their differences in a way that avoids protracted arguments and promotes co-operation between parents in decisions concerning children.

It's also important that you like your solicitor. Make sure it's someone that you feel you can talk to, a person who listens to you and understands where you're coming from. You need to be confident that they'll provide reliable advice and will let you make your own decisions. They should also help you understand the consequences of the decisions that you make.

Many solicitors offer a free first appointment, which can be very useful in establishing whether or not you think you can work with them on an ongoing basis. They will also tell you whether or not you're eligible for help with legal fees through the Community Legal Service (Legal Aid). You might find it helpful to make a list of questions you want to ask and take notes while you're there so you don't forgot anything important.

An increasing number of specialist family lawyers have trained in the 'collaborative model' of resolving disputes (over seven hundred in England and Wales as of January 2007). This can most easily be described as a hybrid between conventional legal negotiations and mediation. It involves the couple *and* their lawyers signing a participation agreement in which they commit to resolving issues based on mutual interests and the welfare of the family as a whole, and also commit not to take their dispute to court. The model encourages couples to identify common interests (for example, the desire to be able to share future family functions without embarrassment) with a view to measuring options for outcome against those common interests: 'Will this proposal help us achieve our common aims?' All work is done in four-way meetings, minimising the need for correspondence between the lawyers. Where other advisers are needed to assist with issues concerning the finances or children, then those third parties are jointly instructed and invited to attend one or more of the four-way meetings. The 'no court rule' encourages a creative and more determined approach to settlement. In the event that negotiations break down, the parties have to appoint new lawyers. It is this that keeps everyone at the table for longer.

RESIDENCE AND CONTACT ARRANGEMENTS

Ideally, you and your ex will be able to agree where the children will live and how often they will see the other parent. But if you are not able to agree on these issues, then the courts will decide. Family law does not look at the 'rights' of parents, instead it talks of 'parental responsibility' for a child. If a child's parents were married when the child was born, both will have parental responsibility for the child. A father who was not married to the child's mother when the child was born, will not automatically have parental responsibility but can get it by entering into a Parental Responsibility agreement with the mother, which is then registered at the Principal Registry. New rules from 1 December 2003 say that a father who is not married to the child's mother will have parental responsibility if he is named as the father on the birth certificate.

The Children Act 1989 is the main piece of legislation dealing with family disputes about children. In family law, what used to be called 'custody' and 'access' are now known as 'residence' and 'contact'. The Children Act says that the child's welfare is the paramount consideration when the courts consider any question in relation to the upbringing of a child. Therefore, the court will apply what is known as the 'welfare checklist' to help it make its decision.

The welfare checklist looks at:

➤ The wishes and feelings of the child (considered in the light of his/her age and understanding).
➤ His/her physical, emotional and educational needs.
➤ The likely effect of any change in his/her circumstances.
➤ His/her age, sex, background and any characteristics that the court considers relevant.
➤ Any harm that he/she has suffered or is at risk of suffering.
➤ How capable each parent is of meeting his/her needs.

An independent child and family reporter may be asked to help you resolve the dispute or to help the court decide. They will spend time with each of the parents, and may also speak to the children to ensure that their wishes and needs are being taken into consideration. It is not the child and family reporter's job to make a decision about where a child should reside or how much contact there should be, but simply to gather all the necessary information that a judge may need to make the decision.

However, the court will not make any order relating to a child unless it is satisfied that this would be better for the child than not making an order.

Gillian Bishop from Resolution explains: 'The ethos of the Children Act is that the parents of a child are the people best placed to make decisions regarding their child. In the vast majority of cases where the court's assistance is sought over children issues it will not actively benefit the child[ren] to have an order made about them. Often disputes arise because of a misunderstanding or out of fear, and it is often the case that agreement can be reached if these issues can be aired at a conciliation hearing. Sometimes parents need to hear words of encouragement about their ability to co-parent, as it is pointed out to them that they share the same hopes and dreams for the children. On other occasions, one parent needs to hear words of reassurance from the other parent in order to allay fears which are disrupting contact. Court orders can sadly sometimes be used as a stick with which to beat the other parent – for example, a delayed return from contact beyond the time specified in the order can escalate a problem and turn it into a crisis for the family.'

If residence has been disputed and a residence order is made in favour of one person, then the court will almost certainly make a contact order so that the non-resident parent knows exactly what their contact rights are. Sometimes residence is not being disputed and only a contact order is needed. A contact order might state direct face-to-face contact time as well as indirect contact, or may suggest that there is only direct contact. Unless the children are at risk, most orders will be for a limited period of time in the hope that parents will be able to resolve the issues between themselves. If they can't, then an order can be reinstated as it is, or amended and reinstated.

Contact and safety

If you have experienced domestic violence and/or abuse then you must make sure your solicitor is aware of this and is someone who is experienced in working with cases such as yours. Your ex may try to ensure that they have contact with your children even if you think that it would be unsafe to do so. Your solicitor is the best person to advise you on how to prevent this, or how to allow contact only in an environment where your children will be safe. That might mean that they can only see the children with another adult supervising, such as a grandparent or trusted friend, or it could be someone from social services. Or they may only be able to see them at a supervised contact centre.

You may also be concerned about your own safety. Evidence suggests that violence and abusive behaviour often escalates during a separation, so it is essential that you take extra steps to ensure your own personal safety. Again, this is something that you should speak to your solicitor about. There are a number of actions that can be taken under the Protection from Harassment Act to help you to feel safe, and if you're ever in any doubt about your safety then ring the police.

FINANCIAL ARRANGEMENTS

The settling of financial matters during a divorce is known as 'ancillary relief'. The law is flexible in this area to enable courts to be fair and base their decisions on the individual circumstances of each case. The main piece of legislation in this area is the Matrimonial Causes Act 1973, which sets out the factors that need to be considered. These are:

➤ The welfare of a child of the family.
➤ The income, earning capacity, property and resources of each person.
➤ The financial needs, obligations and responsibilities of each person.
➤ The standard of living enjoyed by the family before the breakdown of the marriage.
➤ The age of each person and the duration of the marriage.

➤ Any physical or mental disability.
➤ The contribution made by each person to the welfare of the family, including looking after the home and bringing up children.
➤ The conduct of each person, but only if it is so bad it would be unfair to ignore it.
➤ Any serious disadvantage to either person that would be caused by ending the marriage.

Because the court has a wide discretion in applying the law, it is better to avoid the uncertainty of a court hearing. Most people are able to agree how their finances should be split with the help of a solicitor to advise on what's fair, to highlight options and to negotiate on their behalf.

The family home is usually the main asset. Since the children's needs are put first, the first consideration will be ensuring they continue to have a suitable home. The family home may be sold and the proceeds divided between the couple (not necessarily in equal shares). Or the property could be transferred to one partner with the other receiving a greater share of other assets. A less common approach could be to allow one person to stay in the house with the other keeping an interest in the property, receiving their share when it is sold – for example, when the youngest child has finished full-time education.

Ideally financial arrangements will be settled through what's known as a 'clean break'. Gillian Bishop from Resolution says: 'A clean break is preferable where it can be achieved without financial hardship because it enables the parties to draw a line under their married relationship and to move on with their lives and new relationship as separated parents.'

Regardless of what arrangements are made about dividing possessions and household assets between the parents, financial provision for any dependent children is a separate matter. Parents will need to agree how their children will be provided for. Most couples agree a regular amount or percentage of income that will be paid from one parent to the other until the children have left full-time education. This payment is normally referred to as child maintenance or child support. If a figure cannot be agreed then the Child Support Agency (CSA) may be used to calculate the prescribed amount. The CSA must be used if the parent seeking child support is in receipt of state benefits. However, please be aware that the CSA, as it is presently constituted, will be abolished in the next couple of years. There is not enough space in this book to deal with the proposed reforms so you should make sure that you obtain specific advice on this aspect of your case should the need arise.

THE DIVORCE PROCEDURE

Divorce is a legal process, which is carried out by the civil courts. The procedure begins with a petition and ends with a decree absolute, which dissolves the marriage. The timescale to complete the process differs from case to case, but even the most straightforward cases take four to six months. If you have children, then part of the divorce process will include a statement of arrangements for children. This document shows that all the necessary arrangements to look after and financially support the children have been made. Since this is needed before the divorce can be finalised, it's best to have agreed all these details with your ex either alone, through mediation or via solicitors before you begin divorce proceedings.

There is only one 'ground' for divorce and that is that the marriage has irretrievably broken down. This is proved by establishing the existence of one of five factual circumstances. These are:

➤ Your spouse has committed adultery and you find it intolerable to continue to live with him/her.

➤ Your spouse has behaved in such a way that it would be unreasonable to expect you to continue to live with him/her.

➤ Your spouse has deserted you for a continuous period of two years or more.

➤ You have been living apart from your spouse for two years or more and your spouse agrees to the divorce.

➤ You have been living apart from your spouse for five years or more, whether or not your spouse agrees to the divorce.

It is no longer compulsory in a petition based on adultery to name the third person concerned.

The divorce process will be much simpler if both of you have agreed the reasons for the divorce. If a divorce is contested then the procedure can take much longer. In a nutshell, the process is as follows.

The person who starts the divorce, known as the 'petitioner', sends a divorce petition to the other partner, known as the 'respondent', along with a statement of arrangements for children, marriage certificate and a court fee. The petitioner's solicitor then sends a copy of the petition and statement of arrangements to the respondent together with a form of acknowledgement to complete and return within eight days. Assuming they do not disagree and decide to defend the petition, the petitioner's solicitor prepares an affidavit (a sworn statement), which confirms that the contents of the petition are true. This is then sent to the court with a request for a date for pronouncement of the provisional decree of divorce, known as the 'decree nisi'. A judge then looks through the papers, decides if the petitioner is entitled to a divorce, checks the statement of arrangements for children is sufficient and mutually agreed, and certifies that the decree nisi can be pronounced. The petitioner and respondent will be notified of the date of the hearing but they are not required to attend. If the judge is unhappy with the arrangements for children he or she may ask for further information, or ask the petitioner and respondent to attend an informal appointment to clarify and explore areas of concern. A copy of the decree nisi will be sent to both the petitioner and the respondent, and once a minimum of six weeks and one day has passed, the petitioner may apply for decree absolute. Once this is received the marriage is legally dissolved.

If the divorce is defended then the respondent must file a defence, known as an 'answer', and the respective solicitors will attempt to find mutual grounds that are acceptable before reapplying to court. If there is no agreement – for example, where one party does not wish to be divorced – then ultimately a court will determine whether there should be a divorce. However, Gillian Bishop from Resolution warns: 'Defended divorces are held in open court, i.e. they are open to the public and the press. Because they are so rare they make good material for tabloid newspapers. You should think long and hard before subjecting yourself and your family to such publicity.'

COHABITATION AND THE LAW

Sometimes people refer to couples who have been living together, and possibly bringing up children together, over a long period of time as 'common law' husbands and wives. There is, in fact, no such legal status.

The law refers to this sort of relationship as cohabitation. When a couple are not married but cohabiting and then separate, there is no legal provision for maintenance or procedure for dividing property or assets in a fair way. This is a contentious area of the law and one that is currently under review. The new Civil Partnership Bill (2004) has gone some way to changing the situation for same-sex couples but much still needs to be done.

The Law Commission has recently issued a consultancy document on the subject, but it remains to be seen when a change to the law may happen in practice and what that change will be.

If you and your partner had drawn up a cohabitation agreement then you may have more protection, but this is yet to be fully tested in court. Generally speaking, cohabitees have no individual financial claims against their ex-partners. They may have a claim in respect of a shared home, but that will depend on the circumstances. The current law in this area is a real minefield, so you must take legal advice.

Where children are involved, different law applies in relation to them. In these cases the primary carer of the children will be able to bring financial claims *on behalf of the children* under Schedule 1 of the Children Act seeking:

1. One-off capital sums to cover particular child-related expenses – for example, the additional costs that arise when a child is born, the provision of a musical instrument, or a car to enable the parent to take the child places. There is no limit to the number of such applications.
2. A capital sum for the provision of housing for the child.
3. School fees.

The factors that a court will have in mind when assessing such claims are:

a) The welfare of the child(ren).
b) The income, earning capacity, property and resources of each person.
c) The financial needs, obligations and responsibilities of each person.

It should be noted, however, that capital provided for housing is only lent by the paying parent. Once the property is no longer needed as a home, usually when they have finished full-time education, then the contribution is returned with interest to the parent who provided it. Issues of child support are currently dealt with through the CSA (see above).

WHEN LEGAL AGREEMENTS ARE IGNORED

Even when a financial agreement has been reached and child maintenance agreed, or a contact order has been made, there are some parents who will refuse to go along with it. A few may be willing to go to mediation but for many there may be little choice but to go back to the courts to try to get something done. In reality, little can be done as the British legal system is increasingly choked by people ignoring contact orders and financial agreements. Often the reason for this is unresolved anger and bitterness on behalf of one of the partners, and until it subsides they may refuse to play ball, whatever the courts say. Unfortunately, all you can do in these circumstances is return to your solicitor and explore ways of enforcing the order, which can be a lengthy and painful process for all.

Conclusion

As we've seen before, divorce never ends for children. No matter how much time passes, their parents will always be separated. But the pain of divorce does come to an end.

As long as parents reach the place where they can put their divorce in the past and look forward optimistically to their future, then so will their children.

As ten-year-old Stephen wisely said to me, 'It's all about change.' Life is full of changes; some predictable and welcomed, others painful and unwanted. Our task is to adjust to those changes as best we can, and make the most of what life offers us.

As a parent, you have the profound and awesome privilege of teaching your children how relationships should be. Everything you say and do is a lesson for them, one that can teach them love, respect and tolerance – or cynicism and distrust.

No matter what your experience of divorce may have been, or what the future may now hold for you, remember that your relationship with your partner may be over, but your relationship with your kids is for life.

Resources

FOR CHILDREN

Books

Three to seven:
Dinosaurs Divorce: A Guide for Changing Families by Laurence Krasny Brown and Marc Brown (Little, Brown, 1986)

It's Not Your Fault, Koko Bear by Vicki Lansky and Jane Prince (Book Peddlers, 1998)

Under ten:
Two Homes by Claire Masurel and Kady MacDonald Denton (Walker Books, 2002)

Nine to twelve:
What in the World Do You Do When Your Parents Divorce? by Kent Winchester and Roberta Beyer (Free Spirit Publishing, 2001)

Pre-teens and teens:
My Parents Are Getting Divorced: How to keep it together when your mom and dad are splitting up by Florence Cadier (Harry N Abrams, 2004)

The Suitcase Kid by Jacqueline Wilson (Corgi, 2006)

Websites

www.itsnotyourfault.org
Practical information from NCH for children, young people and parents going through a break-up.

www.thehideout.co.uk
A website set up by Women's Aid specifically to help children living with domestic violence.

www.there4me.com
Support and advice from the NSPCC for young people.

www.thesite.org
General advice and support for over 16's from YouthNet UK.

FOR ADULTS

Books

Relate books, especially:
Loving Yourself, Loving Another by Julia Cole (Vermilion, 2001)
Moving On by Suzie Hayman (Vermilion, 2001)
Starting Again by Sarah Litvinoff (Vermilion, 2001)
Staying Together by Susan Quilliam (Vermilion, 2001)
Step Families by Suzie Hayman (Vermilion, 2001)

Divorced Dad's Survival Book: How to stay connected with your kids by David Knox and Kermit Leggett (Da Capo Press, 2000)

Shared Parenting, Raising your children cooperatively after separation by Jill Burrett and Michael Green (Finch Publishing, 2007)

The Other Side of the Closet: The Coming Out Crisis for Straight Spouses and Their Families by Amity Pierce Buxton (John Wiley, 1994)

The Survivor's Handbook (available from Women's Aid)

Websites

www.alcoholconcern.org.uk
A national voluntary agency providing advice and support to anyone concerned with alcohol addiction.

www.childline.org.uk
Provides online and telephone support for children of all ages struggling with a wide range of issues.

www.collabfamilylaw.org.uk
An information site on family law.

www.directgov.gov.uk
A general public service site that provides legal information on separation and divorce.

www.divorceaid.co.uk
An independent group of professionals providing excellent all round advice and support on every aspect of divorce and separation. Also provides resources for children and teenagers.

www.insidedivorce.co.uk
An online information site and services directory covering every aspect of divorce and separation.

www.MIND.org.uk
The UK's national association for mental health.

www.parentlineplus.org.uk
A national charity with decades of experience of supporting parents and carers via a range of free, flexible, innovative services.

www.pinktherapy.com
The UK's largest independent therapy organisation working with gender and sexual minority clients.

www.relate.org.uk
Relate offers advice, relationship counselling, sex therapy, workshops, mediation, consultations and support, face-to-face, by phone and through this website.

www.resolution.org.uk (formerly known as The Solicitors Family Law Association) An organisation of 5,000 family solicitors, who are committed to resolving disputes in a non-confrontational manner.

www.respect.uk.net
National association of domestic violence perpetrators programmes. Provides information and help for perpetrators of domestic violence.

www.stopitnow.org.uk
A public information and awareness-raising campaign regarding childhood sexual abuse.

www.talktofrank.com
A national resource for young people and their carers who need information and advice on drugs and drug related issues.

www.ukcfm.co.uk
The website of the UK College of Family Mediators. Provides information on family mediaton and information on regional mediaton services.

www.womensaid.org.uk
A national domestic violence charity that provides support, advice and temporary accommodation to women and men affected by violence or abuse.

Helplines

National Domestic Violence Helpline (run in partnership by Women's Aid and Refuge)
0808 2000 247

National Mediation Helpline
0845 60 30 809

PACE Family Support Service
0207 700 1323

Parentline Plus
0808 800 222

Relate
0845 456 1310

Index